1 Peter

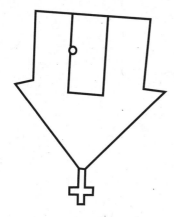

1 Peter

SURPRISED BY
THE CHURCH
JESUS IS BUILDING

J. D. Walt

ZONDERVAN

1 Peter
Copyright © 2024 by J. D. Walt

Published in Grand Rapids, Michigan, by Zondervan. Zondervan is a registered trademark of The Zondervan Corporation, L.L.C., a wholly owned subsidiary of HarperCollins Christian Publishing, Inc.

Requests for information should be addressed to customercare@harpercollins.com.

Zondervan titles may be purchased in bulk for educational, business, fundraising, or sales promotional use. For information, please email SpecialMarkets@Zondervan.com.

ISBN 978-0-310-16222-3 (audio)

Library of Congress Cataloging-in-Publication Data

Names: Walt, J. D. (John David). author.
Title: 1 Peter : surprised by the church Jesus is building / J.D. Walt.
Other titles: First Peter: surprised by the church Jesus is building
Description: Grand Rapids, Michigan : Zondervan Reflective, [2024] | Includes bibliographical references.
Identifiers: LCCN 2023057819 (print) | LCCN 2023057820 (ebook) | ISBN 9780310162209 (paperback) | ISBN 9780310162216 (ebook)
Subjects: LCSH: Bible. Peter, 1st—Meditations. | Spiritual exercises. | BISAC: RELIGION / Christian Living / Spiritual Growth | RELIGION / Christian Living / Devotional
Classification: LCC BS2795.54 .W35 2024 (print) | LCC BS2795.54 (ebook) | DDC 227/.9206—dc23/eng/20240215
LC record available at https://lccn.loc.gov/2023057819
LC ebook record available at https://lccn.loc.gov/2023057820

Cover design and illustrations: Derek Thornton / Notch Design
Interior design: Denise Froehlich

Printed in the United States of America

24 25 26 27 28 LBC 5 4 3 2 1

To my father-farmer, David Walt,
who welcomed me
into the fertile field
of the early morning
and taught me how to sow there
the daily seeds
of the Word of God

Contents

Week 3: 1 Peter 2:9–10

Week 4: 1 Peter 2:11–3:6

Week 5: 1 Peter 3:7–18

Week 6: 1 Peter 3:19–4:7

Week 7: 1 Peter 4:7–16

Week 8: 1 Peter 4:17–5:14

Preface

What are the two most important words of the day? I'm glad you asked. My take: the first word and the last word. Who gets the first word in your day? Who gets the last word? I have a confession: I have realized my slow drift into giving Instagram the first word of my day. It was simple and benign—just a quick scroll through the photos my friends posted over the last half day or so. Then this realization: Netflix was getting the last word of my day. Before drifting off to sleep, I would watch the next episode of some show that had caught my attention along the way. First word: *Instagram*. Last word: *Netflix*.

Days become weeks. Weeks become months. Months become years. And days, weeks, months, and years become us. Our lives consist not in the big decisions and banner events dotting our calendars, but in the little things we consistently do day after day after day. We are what we do . . . every single day.

Each one of us has within our stewardship the ability to decide who will get the first and last words in our life. You know where this is headed. But first let me tell you what happened with my Instagram-Netflix ways. The problem is that I want to make Instagram and Netflix the problem when they aren't the problem. The problem is with me and the misspent priority of my own heart. So I didn't decide to delete Instagram and swear off Netflix. Instead, I decided I would shift the priority of my heart. I determined to give the Word of God the first word and the last word of my days.

Though my day may be filled with a thousand distractions and a hundred course corrections, it is now determined—my day will be framed by, surrounded with, enclosed in the Word of God. First Word. Last Word. God's Word.

The grass withers and the flowers fall,
but the word of our God endures forever.
(Isaiah 40:8)

Consider the stark simplicity and brazen boldness of this word from the prophet Isaiah. Everything is ephemeral. Only one thing is eternal—the Word of God.

Next to the front door of our home, the one we enter and exit through almost every time, is a chalkboard. And on the chalkboard are written those words. I read that verse at least once every single day. I say it aloud so my ears can hear it. Can I possibly be reminded enough that everything around me is passing away save one thing—the Word of God? Can I possibly be encouraged enough to come to Jesus and have him build my life on the singular enduring reality of the Word of God? First Word. Last Word. God's Word.

I offer you an invitation through this book to journey with me and others to shift the priority of your heart and mind. Each day we will gather around a biblical text. We will invite the text of Scripture to speak both the first and the last word of our day. Write some of the text for the day in a journal or on a notecard, a whiteboard, or a chalkboard, and make it a simple act of worship to read it aloud each morning as the first word of the day and also at the close as the last word of the day.

Along the way we will reflect together on how to increase the priority, prominence, and integration of the Word of God in our everyday lives. If we will give ourselves to the gentle work of this way of walking together, I suspect we will find pathways of delight and devotion winding through the wilderness of this world and the sanctuaries of our own souls that we never imagined existed. And something tells me these First-Word-Last-Word-God's-Word paths will find their way into tomorrow and next week and next month and onward, until they have become our lives.

Now I'm going to say, "The grass withers and the flowers fall," and you are going to say, "But the word of our God endures forever."

J. D. WALT

How This Works

This is a different kind of Bible study. The Bible is both the source and the subject. And you will learn information about the Bible along the way, such as its history, context, original languages, and authors. The goal is not educational in nature, but transformational. We will focus more on knowing Jesus than on knowing *about* Jesus.

To that end, each reading begins with the definitive inspiration of the Holy Spirit, the ongoing, unfolding text of Scripture. Following that is a short and hopefully substantive insight into the text and some aspect of its meaning. For insight to lead to deeper influence, we turn the text into prayer. Finally, influence must run its course toward impact. This is why you will find questions at the end of each chapter. These questions are designed not to elicit information but to crystallize intention.

Discipleship always leads from inspiration to attention, from attention to intention, and from intention to action.

Committing to Everyday Reading and Prayer

While Scripture always addresses us personally, it is not written to us individually. The content of Scripture cries out for a community of listeners and readers. This resource is designed for discipleship in community. You could read this like a traditional book—a few pages or chapters at a time. You could cram the readings the night before a group meeting. Those ways of reading are not the intention of this book. Keep in mind, Daily Seeds is not called *Daily* Seeds for kicks. We believe Scripture is worthy of our most focused and consistent attention. Every day. We all have misses, but let's make everyday reading and prayer more than a noble aspiration; let's make it our covenant with one another.

This discipleship tool will create spiritual habits of individual reading and of praying the biblical text—six days on your own and one day with others.

How to Use with Small Groups

Daily Seeds is a proven discipleship resource that works in a variety of contexts—from churches studying a book of the Bible together to small groups to Sunday school classes to virtual meetings. Assuming your group meets weekly, group and class members should read one chapter every day. You will notice there is not an assigned reading for the seventh day. On the seventh day, meet with your group to share, pray, and encourage one another with insights or struggles that the text brought up in you during the previous six days. Use the following guidelines to help structure your group meetings as you allow Scripture to transform you in community.

The guidelines for using Daily Seeds in small groups or class settings are meant to be simple. Perhaps share the responsibility of leading group meetings. Remember that the goal is transformation.

1. Hearing the Text
Invite the group to settle into silence for a period of no less than one and no more than five minutes. Ask an appointed person to keep time and to read the biblical text covering the period of days since the last group meeting. Allow at least one minute of silence following the reading of the text.

2. Responding to the Text
Invite anyone from the group to respond to the reading by answering these prompts: What did you hear? What did you see? What did you otherwise sense from the Lord?

3. Sharing Insights and Implications for Discipleship
Moving in an orderly rotation (or free-for-all), invite people to share insights and implications from the week's readings. What did you find challenging, encouraging, provocative, comforting, invasive, inspiring,

corrective, affirming, guiding, or warning? Allow group conversation to proceed at will. Limit to one sharing item per turn, with multiple rounds of discussion.

4. Shaping Intentions for Prayer

Invite each person in the group to share a single discipleship intention for the week ahead. It is helpful if this goal for growing in discipleship can also be framed as a question the group can use to check in from the prior week. At each person's turn, they are invited to share how their intention went during the previous week. The class or group can open and close the meeting according to its established patterns.

Introduction

Sometimes you meet a person who changes your life forever. You don't realize it at the time; you usually sense it only much later and in retrospect. You remember how that person was just like everyone else, and yet they were different. There was something special about them. It wasn't their big personality. It really wasn't the way you saw them, but the way *they saw you*. These people have a way of being themselves without being about themselves. Their presence conveys a capacity for seeing people, an almost limitless spaciousness for others.

This is who Jesus is and what he's like to be around. Don't believe me? Just ask Peter. His is a story of being seen—and being transformed as a result.

Peter, author of the letter we'll be reading through, was an "unschooled, ordinary" fisherman (Acts 4:13) content to cast his nets on the Sea of Galilee until his brother Andrew introduced him to Jesus. Andrew said to him, "'We have found the Messiah' (that is, the Christ). And he brought him to Jesus" (John 1:41–42).

Pay close attention to what happens next. "Jesus looked at him and said, 'You are Simon son of John. You will be called Cephas' (which, when translated, is Peter)" (John 1:42).

Jesus must have recognized that, while Peter wasn't smart, he was brilliant. He had a heart and mind somehow postured to receive revelation.

Brilliance is another order of intelligence entirely. Brilliance comes from being with Jesus. Brilliance comes from swimming in the stream of divine revelation. Brilliant people are the ones who walk on water. These folks know their utter ordinariness and embrace it. They know they don't need to try to prove anything to anyone or try to be something they are not. They know who they are, because they know in the deepest way that they belong to Jesus.

This should encourage us, because we have a front-row seat on Peter's journey. We know he started out pretty insecure and needy, masquerading as an authority who had it all together. We saw his self-aggrandizing behavior at the Last Supper. And like a train wreck in slow motion, we watched his prodigious collapse on Good Friday. We witnessed his breathtaking restoration by Jesus on the shore of the Sea of Galilee. And now we hold in our hands one of the most significant documents in the history of the world, penned by the hand of an uneducated fisherman.

We are all in the midst of some version of Peter's same journey, struggling to leave behavior management behind and step into the beholding and becoming way of life. Peter was transformed when he met Jesus. He let Jesus become the defining reality of his life. And we can do the same.

When we let Jesus become the defining reality of our lives, our presence will take on his likeness in a way only we can express.

Helping people find transformation in Christ is Peter's goal in writing this letter. Peter wants us to understand who we are, where we are, and what we are doing here. He is orienting us. He's giving us a game plan. He's offering us a vision of the church Jesus is building. He's calling us to wake up, to rise up, to step into the resurrection life Jesus alone offers. He's calling us to become disciples transformed by Jesus into his likeness, ready to transform the world.

Wake up, sleeper, rise from the dead . . .[1]

---

1. Ephesians 5:14.

1
WEEK

---

1 Peter 1:1–12

---

1 Peter 1:1

1 | Exiles

> Peter, an apostle of Jesus Christ,
>   To God's elect, exiles scattered throughout the provinces of
> Pontus, Galatia, Cappadocia, Asia and Bithynia . . .

═══ Consider This ═══

Peter uses the opening lines of his letter to identify the key players: the author—Peter himself, "an apostle of Jesus Christ"—and his audience. He uses several terms to describe his audience, including one we'll examine more closely now: *exiles*.

Who is this?

To be an exile is to be a person or group of people who have been expelled from their country of origin and sent into a foreign land, a place where they are strangers and aliens. Exiles have a home in this world but refuse to make themselves at home in this world.

There are three levels at which we are exiles. In Genesis 3, after the catastrophic incident in the Garden of Eden, Adam and Eve were exiled. Thus began the long journey, beginning again with Abraham and Sarah back toward a garden land, a land flowing with milk and honey, also known as the promised land. It came to fruition in the entry of the Hebrew people into the land we know today as Israel. Unfortunately, through persistent disobedience to the terms of the covenant God made with them, they found themselves in exile again. And just like that, there we were again, a people walking in darkness.

But you know the rest of the story of the people walking in darkness, right?

With the coming of Jesus—Messiah, Light of the World—the prophecy was fulfilled: "On those living in the land of deep darkness a light has dawned" (Isaiah 9:2).

So the exile is over, right? No. We remain in an exilic reality. We are exiles who live in the land of darkness but who walk in the kingdom of light. We are strangers and aliens in a foreign land. Our hearts are set on pilgrimage to the new creation. We are marching to Zion. If we should die before we get there, we shall not perish. Heaven will be our holding place. The future, however, is not somewhere up there. It is here, in the new heaven and the new earth, finally and fully coming with the return of King Jesus, the Messiah.

As the scattered exiles, we understand our citizenship is in the kingdom of heaven. When we gather ourselves on earth, church happens. The kingdom breaks out—on earth as it is in heaven. The blind see, deaf hear, lepers are cleansed, lame walk, dead are raised, poor hear good news.

But, you ask, why aren't we seeing these demonstrations of the kingdom now? Dear friends, as Galadriel said in *The Fellowship of the Ring*, "Much that once was is lost. For none now live who remember it." We have lived through a long period of the history of the church known as Christendom. It is the outcome of the attempted Christianization of society. Much good has come from this era, and yet as it now sits on the threshing floor of history, the chaff seems to overwhelm the grain. Christendom propagated multitudinous forms of church that in many ways obscured and even defied the essence of the kingdom of Jesus. In retrospect, it looks like the failed experiment of the church doing its best to make itself at home in the world. I am grossly oversimplifying this and perhaps even overstating it, but you get the point.

We can't go back to the first few centuries of the church, as many conservative movements have thought possible. We certainly can't reinvent the gospel, as many progressive movements have tried and failed to do. We can only awaken to the simple and comprehensive gospel of Jesus. In fact, every generation must do so—person by person by person. Every time this happens, we see awakening. The greatness of an awakening is determined only by the level of darkness it displaces. Great awakenings tend to be reserved for periods of great darkness.

So, fellow exiles, where do we find ourselves now? Christendom has left the church in a state of deep slumber. We had thought the Christian faith could be delegated to institutions and organizations—that they could somehow be Christian for us—only to learn that only people can be Christians. As a consequence, we, the exilic people of the kingdom of light, are living in a season of great darkness—a season that is spanning our whole lives. For all its wealth and progress, the twentieth century will surely be remembered as among the darkest centuries in human history. Meanwhile, we have seemingly traded in the kingdom for the church industrial complex. We now find ourselves, still early in the twenty-first century, in a world of utter, even absurd confusion. We are now paying the compounding interest of the debts imposed by a seditiously sophisticated and seductive darkness that only persists and grows.

Our temporary home remains in this world. However, we can no longer afford to make ourselves at home in this world. It is time to wake up, exiles. This is not about somehow taking a country back to some earlier age. It is about sowing an eternal kingdom into this earthly soil, releasing the tight grip we have on our comfortable lives in exchange for what Jesus alone can and will do through a people wholeheartedly consecrated to him.

The stakes have never been higher. It is time to sow for a great awakening. We will get the awakening we sow for. So many of us have reaped where we have not sown. It is time to sow where we may not fully reap. Nothing is more worthy of our lives than our determination to sow. Let's go out sowing with all we've got for the sake of generations yet unborn who may reap the harvest.

Wake up, sleeper, rise from the dead . . .

The Prayer

Jesus, you are the Messiah, the Son of the living God. We are exiles in a foreign land, strangers and aliens on pilgrimage. We are looking forward to the city with foundations whose architect and builder is God. Indeed, we are longing for a better country. Holy Spirit, would you break open our hearts that we might be filled with the heart of Jesus? As he was in the world, so are we. Awaken us to the fullness of who you are and to your purposes in our time. Renew your purposes in our day. We pray in Jesus' name. Amen.

The Questions

Are you waking up? There's only one way to know. Is your life becoming a seed of the awakening love of Jesus in the lives of others? Let's go, exiles!

1 Peter 1:2

2 | ## The Fisherman-Theologian

> . . . who have been chosen according to the foreknowledge of God the
> Father, through the sanctifying work of the Spirit, to be obedient to
> Jesus Christ and sprinkled with his blood:
> Grace and peace be yours in abundance.

═══ Consider This ═══

This second little verse packs a punch. In it, we not only get the Father,
Son, and Holy Spirit, but Peter opens the door to the first half and the
second half of the gospel. We get to deal with foreknowledge, sanctification, obedience, and, yes, the blood of Jesus. And to think that when
I read this verse in the past, I just skimmed right by all this, thinking I
already knew it!

No skimming today. Let's examine two important concepts we find
in 1 Peter 1:2: Trinitarian theology and the concept of foreknowledge.

1. The Trinity

Peter, in the span of one sentence—and his first, no less—is already
articulating a full-blown Trinitarian theology. It's crazy when you think
about it. He's a fisherman, for crying out loud! He's not a theologian.
And that's the point. It's time to take back theology from the theologians. Theology belongs to everyone, and in fact, everyone is a theologian
in one sense or another. We are all doing theology.

Some people believe the whole concept of the Trinity was developed much later in Christian history and is, in fact, not biblical, since
the word Trinity never appears in the Bible. But we need only look at
the second verse of Peter's first letter to see how the understanding and
experience of God as Trinity developed rapidly, beginning on the Day
of Pentecost. Behold the triune grammar here:

> . . . according to the foreknowledge of God the Father, through

the sanctifying work of the Spirit, to be obedient to Jesus Christ and sprinkled with his blood.

Father, Son, and Holy Spirit all in the same sentence—and this is one of several examples across the New Testament.

Fishermen don't write theoretical treatises for academic speculation; fishermen write revealed doctrine that turns out to be brimming, even overflowing, with brilliant words, filled with divine grace and truth.

2. Foreknowledge

Let's move on to the second major topic in this verse—foreknowledge. We struggle to grasp the biblical concept of foreknowledge. Something in us wants God's foreknowledge to be determinative and even controlling. So what if God's foreknowledge is not determinative but rather predictive? Here's my thesis: God doesn't control the future as a predetermined outcome. He accurately predicts the future according to how one responds to his Word. I know this may ruffle some feathers, so suspend your judgment while you keep reading.

The Greek word translated here as "foreknowledge" is *prognosin*, from which we get our English word *prognosis*. When a doctor gives a prognosis, they tell you the expected outcome of a disease and the prescribed remedy. Aunt Mildred has cancer. We want to know, "What's the prognosis?" The doctor said they think they caught it early, and they believe that with radiation and some chemotherapy they can beat it. A doctor's foreknowledge or prognosis is tentative and subject to being wrong. The foreknowledge or prognosis of God, while predictive, is a certainty. God the Father gives a prognosis for anyone who will follow Jesus Christ through the power of the Holy Spirit. This person's life will flourish, even—as Peter's letter will show us—in the midst of great difficulty.

═══ The Prayer ═══

Jesus, you are the Messiah, the Son of the living God. Thank you for Peter, who shows us a very ordinary person who understands what revelation is and how it works—how it requires a humility laden with boldness. We confess we have read his words for years and not given much thought to his person, which shows us he doesn't point to himself but to you. Holy Spirit, teach us through this example how to be this kind of a witness. How can we be ourselves without being about ourselves? Praying in Jesus' name. Amen.

The Questions

Did you ever realize how profound this first verse (one sentence) of 1 Peter is? What does this verse reveal about the nature of revelation and how to perceive it? Have you ever thought of yourself as a theologian? It's about time, isn't it?

3

1 Peter 1:3–5

Anybody Remember Black-and-White Television?

Praise be to the God and Father of our Lord Jesus Christ! In his great mercy he has given us new birth into a living hope through the resurrection of Jesus Christ from the dead, and into an inheritance that can never perish, spoil or fade. This inheritance is kept in heaven for you, who through faith are shielded by God's power until the coming of the salvation that is ready to be revealed in the last time.

Consider This

Anybody out there remember black-and-white television programs? They included no color. Even after color television came along, you could still watch a lot of the older black-and-white television programs. Here's the crazy thing: when I watched black-and-white television shows, I assumed the world depicted on the screen was actually black-and-white. It never occurred to me that I was watching a fully colored reality being depicted in black-and-white. I thought that, because all I saw was black-and-white, the reality must actually be black-and-white. I could not possibly picture the world on-screen in color. I wouldn't even try. I just accepted it as it appeared.

This seems to me to be a metaphor for how I have read the Bible for so long. I am so familiar with the Bible as I have known it that it is hard to know anything else. I'm so used to watching it in black-and-white that it doesn't readily occur to me that a lot more may be there than what I have seen. It is the curse of familiarity. I can be so familiar with someone or something that I can only see what I have already seen and be blocked from seeing what is most fully there. Hence the saying, "Familiarity breeds contempt."

As I read 1 Peter, this whole notion reverberates within me. Take a phrase like in today's text:

> In his great mercy he has given us new birth into a living hope through the resurrection of Jesus Christ from the dead.

If I'm honest, it is so easy to see it as a plain black-and-white picture. Words like *mercy, new birth, hope, resurrection*—they just feel like Christian words I have heard before. You know, Christianese or religious talk.

There's something about *this* time though . . . I am waking up. I am turning over the phrase "new birth" and chipping off the familiar barnacles of my doctrinally encrusted understanding. As I do so, hope begins to rise up as a living reality rather than an ethereal concept. To see the picture in a way I have never seen it before requires that I get rid of the black-and-white TV and get a color TV.

But something about knowing that this is Peter's letter is stirring me. I realize just how gripped Peter is by this thing that has happened before his very eyes to the closest friend he has ever known. Jesus died and was resurrected from the dead. This letter explodes and combusts with all the implications of this single fact. Everything. Every single thing has been turned upside down and must be re-seen, re-evaluated, and re-framed by this event. Peter is no longer seeing reality in black-and-white but in a color so vivid he wonders what he was even seeing before and how he had missed it. His pen is on fire with an otherworldly revelation that has landed on earth, on him. All the stuff Jesus said and taught about storing up treasure in heaven is real and true and materializing in full and living color.

> . . . and into an inheritance that can never perish, spoil or fade. This inheritance is kept in heaven for you, who through faith are shielded by God's power until the coming of the salvation that is ready to be revealed in the last time.

Peter is not giving us a doctrine of the new birth. No, he is imparting a revelatory vision. For all its necessity and excellence, doctrine is how we have tried to contain and preserve something that is uncontainable and needs no preservatives. Sometimes, maybe more than sometimes, we need to set aside our preexisting categories and conditions and approach the text with new eyes and the mentality of a beginner, so that we might see the thing to which familiarity has blinded us.

I guess this is what I am asking myself and you: Would you be willing to trade in what you have already seen for what you have yet to see? Might doing so get at what it means to receive a new birth into a living hope through the resurrection of Jesus Christ from the dead and into an inheritance that can never perish, spoil, or fade?

══ The Prayer ══

Jesus, you are the Messiah, the Son of the living God. Thank you for this revelation given to Peter and shared with us. To experience revelation, Lord, this is what we seek: not special revelation but the most uncommon revelation made common to us all—the reality of Jesus Christ, crucified and risen from the dead. We want to turn away from our familiarity and shed it like a coat that doesn't fit anymore. We want to put on the new self, which is being renewed in knowledge in the image of our Creator. Open the eyes of our hearts, Lord; we want to see you. Praying in Jesus' name. Amen.

══ The Questions ══

Would you be willing to trade in what you have already seen for what you have yet to see? What does it mean to you to receive a new birth into a living hope through the resurrection of Jesus Christ from the dead and into an inheritance that can never perish, spoil, or fade?

---

1 Peter 1:6–7

4

There Is Another in the Fire

> *In all this you greatly rejoice, though now for a little while you may have had to suffer grief in all kinds of trials. These have come so that the proven genuineness of your faith—of greater worth than gold, which perishes even though refined by fire—may result in praise, glory and honor when Jesus Christ is revealed.*

═══ Consider This ═══

Let's linger a minute longer in the "black-and-white versus color television" situation. The question is: How can we behold the revealed Word of God? One aspect is like going from black-and-white television to color television. Another aspect is like going from one-dimensional to multidimensional. Jesus Christ, by the Word of God through the Spirit of God, is always working to wake us up from black-and-white to color, from one-dimensional to multidimensional, from one degree of glory to the next. Consider how Paul prays for us to "have power, together with all the Lord's holy people, to grasp how wide and long and high and deep is the love of Christ, and to know this love that surpasses knowledge—that you may be filled to the measure of all the fullness of God" (Ephesians 3:18–19). This is a prayer for an ever-growing capacity to perceive revelation.

The late great Eugene Peterson translated the entire Bible into a present-day vernacular for this very reason—to help us wake up and behold the revealed Word of God and the God of the Word in a fuller dimension of living color. Look how he translates the text we have been working with for the past couple of days:

What a God we have! And how fortunate we are to have him, this Father of our Master Jesus! Because Jesus was raised from the dead, we've been given a brand-new life and have everything to live for, including a future in heaven—and the future starts now! God is keeping careful watch over us and the future. The Day is coming when you'll have it all—life healed and whole. (1 Peter 1:3–5 MSG)

As we behold the revealed Word of God in the person of Jesus Christ, and as he teaches us through the pages of Holy Scripture, we move from flatness to fullness. We move from the flatness of forensic doctrine (which so easily drifts into dogmatism) into the fullness of dynamic relationship together inside the fellowship of Father, Son, and Holy Spirit—and all right here and right now in this world, in the midst of its present darkness. That's what today's text is all about.

> In all this you greatly rejoice, though now for a little while you may have had to suffer grief in all kinds of trials. These have come so that the proven genuineness of your faith—of greater worth than gold, which perishes even though refined by fire—may result in praise, glory and honor when Jesus Christ is revealed.

Now Peter makes the move to encourage us. He sees us in our present situations. He knows we are not only riding the struggle bus much of the time but even spending a fair amount of time under that bus. We "suffer grief in all kinds of trials"—cancer, bankruptcy, divorce, lost jobs, unthoughtful family members, hurtful so-called friends, untimely deaths of loved ones, COVID-19 and 20 and 21 and 22! You get it—all kinds of trials. As soon as one challenge seems to be over, another one is spinning up.

Peter wants us to know that Jesus sees us and what we are going through. Jesus wants us to know that though we feel like we are losing much of the time, it is actually a sign we are winning. This is quite literally the story of Peter's life. Here's the revelation of the day: faith under fire becomes a furnace of transformation.

Speaking of furnaces, do you remember the three amigos—Shadrach, Meshach, and Abednego? It's worth your time to read the whole story, but I'll cut to the chase. They went through a terrible trial that was looking like it would end in their deaths. King Nebuchadnezzar had the three men bound and thrown into a blazing furnace heated seven times its normal heat. We will pick up the text here:

> Then King Nebuchadnezzar leaped to his feet in amazement and asked his advisers, "Weren't there three men that we tied up and threw into the fire?"
>
> They replied, "Certainly, Your Majesty."
>
> He said, "Look! I see four men walking around in the fire, unbound and unharmed, and the fourth looks like a son of the gods." (Daniel 3:24–25)

We know who that fourth person in the furnace was, don't we? Yep—Jesus. Jesus is with you in the trial, and he is taking all that was meant for bad and turning it to good. The fire will seem to destroy you. Do not be afraid; it is only refining you. Cling to Jesus. Here's what he is saying to you today: *You are of greater worth than gold.*

The Prayer

Jesus, you are the Messiah, the Son of the living God. Thank you for your Word in living color, in full dimension, ever stretching the confines of our imagination with how high and wide and deep and long is the vastness of your love. Awaken us to fathom it and make us aware of your presence with us in the trial, standing in the flames and causing them to purify and refine without destroying. Praying in Jesus' name. Amen.

The Questions

What trials are you in the midst of right now? Are you experiencing the grief of it all? Are you ready to give up? Are you looking for relief in all the wrong places? Get still and say these words to Jesus right now: "Jesus, I belong to you." Say them until you are praying them.

5

1 Peter 1:8–9

Why We Don't Really Experience the Inexpressible and Glorious Joy of Our Salvation

> *Though you have not seen him, you love him; and even though you do not see him now, you believe in him and are filled with an inexpressible and glorious joy, for you are receiving the end result of your faith, the salvation of your souls.*

=== **Consider This** ===

Though you have not seen him . . . True.
    you love him . . . True.
    and even though you do not see him now, you believe in him . . . True.
    and are filled with an inexpressible and glorious joy . . . Hmm.

Why the hesitation on that last one? Well, inexpressible and glorious joy—that is over the top. Or is it? This is the common inheritance of every follower of Jesus, and yet it is a quite uncommon reality. When was the last time you saw someone who was exhibiting an inexpressible and glorious joy? When was the last time you had this experience? Why is this? It comes down to the next verse:

> for you are receiving the end result of your faith, the salvation of your souls.

In the present age, the vast majority of Christians do not have a biblical understanding of salvation. We tend to see salvation as something that happened in the past that ensures something that will happen in the future (i.e., going to heaven). This understanding is not entirely wrong—just woefully incomplete. So what is the biblical understanding of salvation?

We have been saved. We are being saved. We will be saved. And there we have the first, second, and third halves of the gospel (see what I did there?). Most Christians only have an understanding of the first half and the third half of the gospel. Salvation was something that happened in their past—when they walked an aisle or got baptized or raised their hand. They got saved. They have a forensic or legal grasp of the gospel. It is salvation as transaction. And the first half of the gospel transaction guarantees the third half of the gospel—transition into heaven when they die.

Salvation is a past event. Salvation is a future event. But the missing link for most Christians is the notion of salvation as a present and ongoing experience. It is this present experience that leads to being filled with an inexpressible and glorious joy. Salvation in the past inspires gratitude. Salvation in the future inspires hope. Gratitude and hope, great as they are, do not rise to the extraordinary level of inexpressible and glorious joy. It is salvation in the present in the midst of the vicissitudes of life that fills one with inexpressible and glorious joy. The text points us to salvation as a present and ongoing experience as the source of the inexpressible and glorious joy. See for yourself:

> . . . and are filled with an inexpressible and glorious joy, for you are receiving the end result of your faith, the salvation of your souls.

Peter didn't say "received," nor did he say "will receive." He said "are receiving." It's why the second half of the gospel is the linchpin of the whole gospel. The end result of the initial transaction is actually being pulled back from the future into the present moment. It is the lived experience of "on earth as it is in heaven." The second half of the gospel is the right here, right now, supernaturally abiding presence of Jesus Christ in us. This is the mystery and the miracle mostly missing from the life of the average Christian. No one has taught and trained us in the transformational realism of what it means to be continuously saved—to receive the sanctifying grace of Jesus rather than be bound to the slavish striving to change our behavior and manage our appearance. This is the second half of the gospel.

Peter, through his letters, is going to coach us up into the second half of the gospel. That's where we are headed.

Jesus, you are the Messiah, the Son of the living God. I want this inexpressible and glorious joy. I am thankful for the forgiveness of my sins. I am confident in an eternal future with you in heaven and later in the new creation. But what I want most of all is to know you more today, to live and move and have my being in you, to be filled by the Holy Spirit with all the fullness of joy. Yes, Jesus, we are saved. We will be saved. But the inexpressible and glorious joy is that we are right here and right now being saved completely and to the uttermost. Yes, Father, more of this. Praying in Jesus' name. Amen.

The Questions

Take a minute to identify for yourself the first half, the second half, and the third half of the gospel. Are you grasping the essential and yet largely missing link of the second half of the gospel?

6

1 Peter 1:10–12

Concerning This Salvation

Concerning this salvation, the prophets, who spoke of the grace that was to come to you, searched intently and with the greatest care, trying to find out the time and circumstances to which the Spirit of Christ in them was pointing when he predicted the sufferings of the Messiah and the glories that would follow. It was revealed to them that they were not serving themselves but you, when they spoke of the things that have now been told you by those who have preached the gospel to you by the Holy Spirit sent from heaven. Even angels long to look into these things.

Consider This

Concerning this salvation . . .

What exactly is *this salvation*?

As I have been saying, this salvation is not the weak-signal, black-and-white television kind of "fire insurance policy, and ticket to heaven" understanding I grew up with in the church. This salvation is thick and robust, totalizing and comprehensive, and fullness beyond fullness in infinitely pixelated color.

This salvation is not just something that happened in the past or that will happen in the future, but it is a miraculous mystery that is manifesting in the right here, right now lives of ordinary saints every single day.

This salvation doesn't begin with original sin but with original glory. It doesn't begin with the fall from grace but with the glory of Eden. It doesn't begin with the problem of sin but with the power of God. Before there was ever a sinner, there was already a Savior.

This salvation is full-court formation to new creation, "as it was in the beginning, is now, and ever shall be: world without end. Amen."[1] It does not end with a disembodied heaven but with the resurrection of the dead in a new heaven and a new earth.

This salvation does not just save sinners from the penalty of sin; it delivers saints from the power of sin. This salvation is comprehensive, full-throated, sin-has-lost-its-power-and-death-has-lost-its-sting transformation.

This salvation recognizes that you are created in the image of Almighty God. Darkness corrupted and sin distorted this image beyond recognition, but grace restores it utterly and completely.

And let's be clear: Sin is darkness and destruction. It's devastating and decimating. It cost God everything, which is why Jesus paid everything to reconcile to himself everything by making peace through his blood shed on the cross. But let's remember: sin did not get the first word, and it shall not get the last.

This salvation is not merely a spiritual solution. This salvation is the totalizing cure, as in the blind see, deaf hear, lame walk, lepers are cleansed, dead are raised, poor hear good news.

This salvation is not just about forgiveness, but about freedom.

---

1. From the Gloria Patri, a short doxology of praise to the Trinity.

This salvation is not just about pardon, but about power.

This salvation is not just about escaping hell in the future, but about embracing the eternal heaven right here and right now on earth.

This salvation is not just Jesus and me, but also the body of Christ and the communion of saints, bound together and enfolded in the extravagant embrace of Father, Son, and Holy Spirit.

This salvation has been long awaited, eagerly sought, suffered for, patiently expected, and now revealed.

> It was revealed to them that they were not serving themselves but you, when they spoke of the things that have now been told you by those who have preached the gospel to you by the Holy Spirit sent from heaven.

Is it any wonder angels long to look into these things?

Isn't it time we looked a lot longer and more deeply into this salvation ourselves?

Wake up, sleeper, rise from the dead . . .

══ The Prayer ══

Jesus, you are the Messiah, the Son of the living God. You are the salvation of heaven, the image of God, the hope of the world. You are rescuer and redeemer, Savior and Lord. Increase our comprehension of this salvation. Take it out of the thin and anemic understanding that has for too long concealed your glory. Bring us into the fullness of understanding, that we might abandon ourselves to you wholeheartedly and completely. This is our one life, Jesus. Only you can make it all it was meant to be, now and forever. Holy Spirit, make it so. Praying in Jesus' name. Amen.

══ The Questions ══

In what way has your vision of "this salvation" been limited by the scope of the problem of sin instead of broadened by the spectacular span of the glory, greatness, and goodness of God?

Week 1:
Discussion Questions

Hearing the Text: 1 Peter 1:1–12

Peter, an apostle of Jesus Christ,

To God's elect, exiles scattered throughout the provinces of Pontus, Galatia, Cappadocia, Asia and Bithynia, who have been chosen according to the foreknowledge of God the Father, through the sanctifying work of the Spirit, to be obedient to Jesus Christ and sprinkled with his blood:

Grace and peace be yours in abundance.

Praise be to the God and Father of our Lord Jesus Christ! In his great mercy he has given us new birth into a living hope through the resurrection of Jesus Christ from the dead, and into an inheritance that can never perish, spoil or fade. This inheritance is kept in heaven for you, who through faith are shielded by God's power until the coming of the salvation that is ready to be revealed in the last time. In all this you greatly rejoice, though now for a little while you may have had to suffer grief in all kinds of trials. These have come so that the proven genuineness of your faith—of greater worth than gold, which perishes even though refined by fire—may result in praise, glory and honor when Jesus Christ is revealed. Though you have not seen him, you love him; and even though you do not see him now, you believe in him and are filled with an inexpressible and glorious joy, for you are receiving the end result of your faith, the salvation of your souls.

Concerning this salvation, the prophets, who spoke of the grace that was to come to you, searched intently and with the greatest care, trying to find out the time and circumstances to which the Spirit of Christ in them was pointing when he predicted the sufferings of the Messiah and the glories that would follow. It was revealed to them that they were not serving themselves but you, when they spoke of the things that have now been told you by those who have preached the gospel to you by the Holy Spirit sent from heaven. Even angels long to look into these things.

Responding to the Text

- What did you hear?
- What did you see?
- What did you otherwise sense from the Lord?

Sharing Insights and Implications for Discipleship

Drawing from the Scripture text and daily readings, what did you find challenging, encouraging, provocative, comforting, invasive, inspiring, corrective, affirming, guiding, or warning?

Shaping Intentions for Prayer

Write your discipleship intention for the week ahead.

2
WEEK

---

1 Peter 1:13–2:8

---

1 Peter 1:13–16

8 | The Real Meaning of Holiness

> *Therefore, with minds that are alert and fully sober, set your hope on the grace to be brought to you when Jesus Christ is revealed at his coming. As obedient children, do not conform to the evil desires you had when you lived in ignorance. But just as he who called you is holy, so be holy in all you do; for it is written: "Be holy, because I am holy."*

Consider This

How did holiness get such a bad rap?

The word usually gets associated with people who are über-religious, dour, prudish, judgmental, or otherwise—the kind of Christians no one would ever want to be.

Everything I just described has absolutely less than nothing to do with holiness. So what exactly is holiness? This is one of those places where the Sunday school answer is exactly right: Jesus.

Holiness is Jesus. All of his ordinary human nature and all of his extraordinary divine nature, and all of this inextricably intertwined together in an indivisible mystical union—holiness is Jesus. And because holiness is Jesus, it should have the best possible reputation we can imagine.

Holiness . . . It's Jesus wrapped in strips of cloth and placed in a feeding trough because there was no room in the inn.

Holiness . . . It's Jesus standing in the river with his cousin, hearing the voice of his Father saying, "My Son. My beloved. With you I am well pleased."

Holiness . . . It's Jesus saying things like "Love your enemies," and "Pray for those who persecute you."

Holiness . . . It's Jesus contributing somewhere around 750 bottles of fine wine to a wedding party run dry.

Holiness . . . It's Jesus breaking all the religious regulations and driving out demons on the Sabbath in the synagogue.

Holiness . . . It's Jesus showing up at a magic fountain to heal a man who had been waiting thirty-eight years for a cure.

Holiness . . . It's Jesus filling two boats to overflowing with fish for fishermen who fished all night and caught nothing.

Holiness . . . It's Jesus putting his healing hands on a leper when a simple word would have sufficed.

Holiness . . . It's Jesus showing up for dinner at a banquet room filled with tax collectors and every other kind of person who had been canceled by the culture.

Holiness . . . It's Jesus walking on water and later filling a bowl with water and washing his disciples' dirty feet.

Holiness . . . It's Jesus forever sharing his reputation with people who had forever ruined theirs.

Holiness . . . It's Jesus mocked, stripped, rebuked, beaten, and crucified, saying, "Father, forgive them. They do not know what they are doing."

Holiness . . . It's Jesus raised from the dead, brandishing radiant scars and unlimited redemption.

Holiness . . . It's Jesus seated at the right hand of the throne of God, pouring out the Spirit of holiness on all who will receive him, and making them uncannily and irresistibly holy as he is holy.

The Prayer

Jesus, you are the Messiah, the Son of the living God. You are the Holy One of God. There is none like you, and yet you have so shared yourself with us that anyone can become like you. Thank you for showing us what holiness most truly is—for cutting through all the pretense and posturing and hypocrisy and showing us that holiness is love and love is holiness. That's what we want. The holiness that is you. It's what we long for. It's all we need. Holy Spirit, make it so. Praying in Jesus' name. Amen.

The Questions

What has been your understanding of holiness? Why? How is that view changing and growing?

1 Peter 1:17–21

9

On the Self-Deceived Nature of Self-Deception

> Since you call on a Father who judges each person's work impartially, live out your time as foreigners here in reverent fear. For you know that it was not with perishable things such as silver or gold that you were redeemed from the empty way of life handed down to you from your ancestors, but with the precious blood of Christ, a lamb without blemish or defect. He was chosen before the creation of the world, but was revealed in these last times for your sake. Through him you believe in God, who raised him from the dead and glorified him, and so your faith and hope are in God.

═══ Consider This ═══

This is a very big story.

And as big as this story is, it is striking to think just how small our part is in it.

But we should not confuse the smallness of our part with its value and significance. We play a very small part in a very big story in a super-significant way.

The history of the world is littered with so many of our ancestors who gave all they had to play a super-magnified and ultimately insignificant part of the infinitesimally small story of their own lives.

That is what today's text refers to as "the empty way of life."

A life filled with self-will, self-rule, self-interest, and self-advancement is an empty way of life. And, yes, there is a way of an apparently others-oriented life that remains quite self-interested.

Perhaps the most broken part of our broken human nature is just how hopelessly self-deceived we are. How else can we account for the levels of sheer chaos in this world? Self-deception compounds like inflationary interest until it creates a debt that cannot possibly be repaid. Perhaps the greatest collective self-deception is that there is some kind of collective solution like communism or socialism or even capitalism. There is only a personal solution. We don't want this to be true, but unfortunately it is, and we can live out our entire lives trapped within our broken selves in an empty way of life. The craziest thing about self-deception is that we have no idea of it when we are self-deceived. And it's in this kind of enslaved condition that we are most apt to isolate ourselves from other people.

There is very good news though. There is a solution to this problem. It is not a collective solution built on ideological foundations or any form of idealism. It is a personal solution with profound social implications because it is not built on an individualized sense of identity. Jesus comes to us personally, even intimately, and yet always in our relatedness to each other. Jesus doesn't offer us a self-improvement program. He offers a very different kind of community. I don't want to call it "the church," because that is all too often just another collectively self-deceived, human-built organization. Remember what Jesus called it that day when Peter famously got it right about Jesus? Let's remember it together:

"But what about you?" he asked. "Who do you say I am?"

Simon Peter answered, "You are the Messiah, the Son of the living God."

Jesus replied, "Blessed are you, Simon son of Jonah, for this was not revealed to you by flesh and blood, but by my Father in heaven. And I tell you that you are Peter, and on this rock I will build my church, and the gates of Hades will not overcome it." (Matthew 16:15–18)

Did you catch it—what Jesus called this new thing he was doing in the world? Yes! He didn't call it the church; he called it "my church." "My church" is not a new community. It is certainly not a new organization. It is a new humanity being built on a regenerated personal and corporate relational union with God—Father, Son, and Holy Spirit.

It always starts with Jesus moving personally to me, and almost immediately it moves to you. Or it starts with Jesus moving personally to you and moves almost immediately to me. And that's why Jesus begins by talking about Peter's faith and his church—a blood-purchased collection of broken people becoming a radiant community of beautiful saints.

This man. This God. This God-Man redeemed us with his very own blood. Wherever there is new birth into a living hope, there will be blood. It is just that costly. Gold and silver can never touch it. Jesus comes right into the cells of our inmost selves, the places where we are hopelessly locked up and so utterly deceived that we have made ourselves at home there—surviving in slavery, mistaking shackles for bracelets, mirrors for windows, and our small stories for the Big Story. And he whispers to some and shouts to others, "Follow me! The door is open."

Peter now brings us Gentile Christians into the Big Story by remembering the exodus and the deliverance of God's people from slavery through the Passover lamb—the night every Hebrew family sacrificed an unblemished perfect lamb and spread its blood over the doorframe of their home so they would be delivered from the plague of death and the slavery of Egypt and into life and freedom. Jesus is our Passover Lamb, and he sets us free from sin, death, and the self-deceptive slavery to ourselves. He actually liberates us into the new humanity of the new creation and empowers us to live there in total freedom, peace, joy, and love.

That's where this letter is headed, so buckle up. The new exodus may get bumpy—especially the upcoming parts where the movement becomes about deliverance from the all too often self-deceived organizations we call "our churches" into the community Jesus calls "my church."

It's why we must keep reminding one another:

Wake up, sleeper, rise from the dead . . .

The Prayer

Jesus, you are the Messiah, the Son of the living God. You are the head of the body, which is what makes it not our church but your church—"my church," you called it. Holy Spirit, grace us to return to Jesus with our whole heart. Lord Jesus, restore us to the Big Story you are writing and our small and significant part to play. Deliver us from the smallness of our own big story and our hopelessly deceived self-interest. Only you can do this. It's why we are praying in your name, Jesus. Amen.

What is your own sense of your self-deception quotient? Zero would be "I can see clearly now," and ten would be "I have no idea what you're even talking about."

---

1 Peter 1:22–25

10   The Great Awakening

> *Now that you have purified yourselves by obeying the truth so that you have sincere love for each other, love one another deeply, from the heart. For you have been born again, not of perishable seed, but of imperishable, through the living and enduring word of God. For,*
>   *"All people are like grass,*
>   *and all their glory is like the flowers of the field;*
>   *the grass withers and the flowers fall,*
>   *but the word of the Lord endures forever."*
> *And this is the word that was preached to you.*

===== **Consider This** =====

Today's set of verses covers three pretty heavy topics—topics we tend to misunderstand: purity, obedience, and love. We frequently examine these topics in isolation, but Peter challenges us to view them as a unit. He shows us how these topics are interconnected: from obedience comes purity of heart, and from purity of heart comes love for each other. Let's spend some time walking through these verses step-by-step, topic-by-topic.

> Now that you have purified yourselves . . .

These six words seem to put the onus on the believer to clean themselves up. The gospel is just the opposite. We present ourselves to God, just as we are, and God cleanses us. And this is not a mere moral kind of cleansing, as in "I need to be cleansed of my bad behavior." The issue is the heart—the seat of our affections and dispositions. The issue is not our unkindness, impatience, jealousy, lust, or anger—or any of the things that present themselves as our problem. Those are merely the symptoms.

We see this same Greek word *hagnidzō* (pronounced hag-**nid**-zō) for *purify* in James 4:8, which reads, "Come near to God and he will come near to you. Wash your hands, you sinners, and purify your hearts, you double-minded." Note the order there.

We have all tried hard to be patient and kind and pure and all the things we know we need to be, yet we still struggle because we are working at the level of the symptoms rather than the heart. Jesus works at the heart level. He treats the sickness, not the symptoms. In other words, NyQuil doesn't cure strep throat. You are going to need a Z-Pak (for our global family, a Z-Pak is shorthand for a particular antibiotic medication). The Word of God is the deep medicine. Jesus is the Great Physician.

> Now that you have purified yourselves by obeying the truth . . .

We have such a preexisting concept of obedience that it is again quite easy to miss the sense of the biblical notion of obedience. We tend to carry a negative connotation of the word *obey* because we immediately associate it with authoritarianism, which is the notion of an authority figure powering down on us—that is, "Don't ask questions. Just do what I say."

The Greek term for obedience, *hypakōe* (pronounced hoop-a-**ko**-ay), means in the most literal sense "under" (*hypo*) and "hear" (*akouō*)—"to hear while sitting under." You recognize the term *acoustics* as coming from this Greek root. Obedience is all about hearing. So to obey the truth means to sit under the sound of truth, "to hear while sitting under."

Obedience does not mean compliant submission to an authoritarian leader; rather, it means a deep kind of submissive listening to the authority of the Truth—which is the Word of God and the God of the Word. Before obedience ever takes a step, it sits down. Before the first hint of activity, it is surrendered attention.

This is what is so remarkable about Jesus. Over and over in

Scripture, the people speak of him as having an astonishing authority that is nothing like the authority of the religious leaders of the day.

Also fascinating is how the Word of God repeatedly references Jesus not as a mere teacher of the truth but as the Truth personified—as the one who is "full of grace and truth" (John 1:14).

One more bit here. Remember the time Jesus visited the home of Mary, Martha, and Lazarus in Bethany? This was the time Martha was so busy trying to get everything ready for everybody. Look what is said concerning Mary: "She had a sister called Mary, who sat at the Lord's feet listening to what he said" (Luke 10:39). Jesus would go on to say, "Mary has chosen what is better" (verse 42).

We are sitting at the feet of Jesus, under his authority, listening to his Word, and the Holy Spirit is training us to stand under and understand his ways. We sit under. Then we stand under. Then we walk under the Light.

The Word of God by the Spirit of God according to the love of God prunes, purifies, cleans, and sets us free for a life of love that becomes so pure (over time) that it actually rises to the level of supernatural power.

> Now that you have purified yourselves by obeying the truth so that you have sincere love for each other, love one another deeply, from the heart.

My friends, this right here is the meaning of life: Love one another deeply, from the heart, with sincere love. Here's the fascinating part. The first instance of the word *love* ("love one another deeply") comes from the Greek term *philadelphia*, which means "brotherly love." The second instance of *love* ("sincere love") derives from the Greek term *agapē*, which means, in essence, the pure love of God. Jesus helps us understand what this kind of love is in John 15:

> "As the Father has loved me, so have I loved you. Now remain in my love. If you keep my commands, you will remain in my love, just as I have kept my Father's commands and remain in his love. I have told you this so that my joy may be in you and that your joy may be complete." (John 15:9–11)

And then he brings it down to the one thing—the very essence and meaning of life itself: "My command is this: Love each other as I have loved you" (verse 12).

This is what it means to love one another deeply from the heart with sincere love—to love each other with the substance and depth of the love of God. This is where it all comes together into a holy, roaring fire: pureheartedness, obedience to the truth, love, abiding, all of it.

"Greater love has no one than this: to lay down one's life for one's friends" (verse 13).

This doesn't necessarily mean to die (unless it *comes* to mean that). It means to release your grip on yourself and your self-interest so much so that you have forgotten yourself. It means to have a pure heart. When human beings do this, people see God. Why? Because only God can do this. "Blessed are the pure in heart, for they will see God" (Matthew 5:8). And therein lies the whole point. It is not the self-interested obedience of compliance; it is the self-forgetful obedience of love. There is nothing more glorious on this side of heaven because this is heaven on this side.

This is the great awakening.

Do you long for it?

The Prayer

Jesus, you are the Messiah, the Son of the living God. You are the truth. You are the Word made flesh. It is such a relief to know that we do not have to figure all this out ourselves, that you are teaching us, as long as we will merely sit at your feet and listen to your Word. It is such a relief to know we don't have to purify ourselves, that you actually purify us by your Word and Spirit. We need only sit in your presence and stand under your Word. Holy Spirit, reorient us away from all our striving and to the place of surrendered sitting with the source. Praying in Jesus' name. Amen.

The Questions

Are you ready to shift away from the busyness of Christian activity and find yourself back at the feet of Jesus, sitting under real authority, listening intently to the deep truth of the Word of God, and trusting his active and powerful presence to do the real work? What will it take to simply get you to the source?

11

1 Peter 2:1–3

From Replacement to Displacement

> *Therefore, rid yourselves of all malice and all deceit, hypocrisy, envy, and slander of every kind. Like newborn babies, crave pure spiritual milk, so that by it you may grow up in your salvation, now that you have tasted that the Lord is good.*

═══ Consider This ═══

Something very powerful is at work in today's text. I think it speaks to the very essence of the Christian faith.

We tend to come at the Christian faith with what I call a replacement theory. It is the replacement of bad behavior with good behavior. It's very easy to read today's text in such a fashion. Look how it opens.

STOP! QUIT! DON'T! BEHAVE!

It's why we need to pay close attention to the first word—*Therefore*. You know the key hermeneutical question, "What is it there for?" Look back to 1 Peter 1:23: "For you have been born again, not of perishable seed, but of imperishable, through the living and enduring word of God." Translation: The miracle has happened. Everything has changed. The center of gravity has shifted. It is like a total restart (that is, new birth).

Still, the typical way the Christian faith gets translated is "believe and behave." The problem? This approach just does not align with the Christian faith; it leads to a religion of conformity. The Christian faith is transcendent transformation. The move is not from believe to behave. It is from believe to behold, and the outcome is far more powerful than behavioral change. The result is becoming a completely new kind of human being.

The key is where Peter goes with verse 2:

> Like newborn babies, crave pure spiritual milk, so that by it you may grow up in your salvation . . .

What does a nursing baby do with its mother? The same thing a mother does with her newborn baby. They behold one another. So it is in our relationship with Jesus. We behold him. He beholds us. We become profoundly bonded together. We "crave pure spiritual milk" (that is, the Word of God). In this way the miracle continues. We behold and we become. This is how we learn to love—by being loved.

Herein lives the beautiful mystery of the Christian faith. The way of the gospel is not replacement of bad behavior with good behavior. The way is displacement of an old life with a new life. The more we focus on behavior, the more that behavior will hold us in its grip. The more we behold Jesus, the more Jesus will hold us in his grip. His presence begins to actually displace our problems. It's why Peter urges us to "crave pure spiritual milk." Why? "So that by it you may grow up into your salvation," which is to say, the lives we were made for—lives of incredible and powerful love for others and glory for God.

Let's leave it where Peter leaves it today:

> . . . now that you have tasted that the Lord is good.

═══ The Prayer ═══

Jesus, you are the Messiah, the Son of the living God. Could this really be true? We don't have to change ourselves. You actually grow us up into your likeness as we give our lives to you. You give us your new life in exchange for our old lives. You aren't calling us to the endless striving to replace the bad with the good. You want to displace the old with the new. Holy Spirit, you are welcome here. Bring the new. Grow me up into this life of salvation. Lead me to crave the pure spiritual milk of the Word of God. Take me to this place of deep, bonded beholding of one another. Praying in Jesus' name. Amen.

Do you feel as though you missed this message somewhere along the way? How can you pick it up now? Not replacement, but displacement. Does it ring true? How does it change your view of sin and repentance?

---

1 Peter 2:4–6

12

Did the Church Leave the Building?

> As you come to him, the living Stone—rejected by humans but chosen by God and precious to him—you also, like living stones, are being built into a spiritual house to be a holy priesthood, offering spiritual sacrifices acceptable to God through Jesus Christ. For in Scripture it says:
>
> > "See, I lay a stone in Zion,
> >> a chosen and precious cornerstone,
> > and the one who trusts in him
> >> will never be put to shame."

===== **Consider This** =====

From the dawn of civilization, people have wanted to define themselves by their buildings. Something about us loves buildings, and something in us wants to define ourselves by our building projects. It's interesting how buildings are a prominent way people want to make a name for themselves (even naming them for themselves). It's nothing new. Does the Tower of Babel ring a bell?

> Then they said, "Come, let us build ourselves a city, with a tower that reaches to the heavens, so that we may make a name for ourselves; otherwise we will be scattered over the face of the whole earth." (Genesis 11:4)

How about the Taj Mahal, Notre-Dame, the World Trade Center, the White House, the Pentagon, the Eiffel Tower? And on and on we could go. People define themselves by their buildings—right down to the homes we live in. Our text today alludes to the most significant building in the history of the world—the temple, which is the symbolic and real dwelling place of the presence of the true and living God in Jerusalem up until the crucifixion, resurrection, and ascension of Jesus Messiah.

The big problem with the temple came about because of the way people learned to go to the temple without going to God. They were going to *get* something from God rather than *give* themselves to God. This twisted purpose effectively turned the place into a den of thieves.

This is yet another of the infinitely amazing things about Jesus. He speaks of a building, but the building materials are the people themselves—living stones. The people are being built together into a spiritual house. Here's the most interesting part. There is only one way into the building.

> As you come to him, the living Stone—rejected by humans but chosen by God and precious to him . . .

Step 1: We come to Jesus. Step 2: Jesus builds us into those who have a deep, abiding connection with other people who have come to him.

> . . . you also, like living stones, are being built into a spiritual house to be a holy priesthood, offering spiritual sacrifices acceptable to God through Jesus Christ.

It seems like we have it exactly backward. More often than not, what is our approach? Step 1: Come to church. Step 2: Come to Jesus.

It's the same problem the ancient people of God had with the temple: Step 1. Come to the temple. Step 2. Come to God. The problem is how the temple gets substituted for God and, similarly and by extension, how the church gets substituted for Jesus. The temple without God is a den of thieves. And coming to church without coming to Jesus? Could it be the same thing? At least we can say the church has left the building. Which might lead us to ask, "Where did it go?"

Jesus, you are the Messiah, the Son of the living God. You are the head of the body, the church. Forgive us for getting it mixed up. Would you take all our groups gathering in all our buildings and do a restart for us? Would you create some defining moments when we can, each one of us, "come to you, the Living Stone," or just stop wasting your time and our time and everyone else's? Break the ruts of our systems and structures and come build your church atop our ruins. We need a level set. It's another way of saying we need a great awakening. Holy Spirit, the living mortar, lead us into this new house of living stones. Praying in Jesus' name. Amen.

══ The Questions ══

Are you seeing the difference between "coming to church" and "coming to Jesus" and how we can do the former and miss the latter? What might it look like if we thought of "joining Jesus" instead of the more typical "joining the church"?

13

1 Peter 2:7–8

I Don't Build My Life; I Surrender It

> *Now to you who believe, this stone is precious. But to those who do not believe,*
>
> > *"The stone the builders rejected*
> >
> > *has become the cornerstone,"*
>
> *and,*
>
> > *"A stone that causes people to stumble*
> >
> > *and a rock that makes them fall."*
>
> *They stumble because they disobey the message—which is also what they were destined for.*

Consider This

It is widely believed the apostle Peter was the eyewitness and chief story-teller behind the gospel of Mark. I wonder if Peter was remembering a particular day at the temple with Jesus:

> As Jesus was leaving the temple, one of his disciples said to him, "Look, Teacher! What massive stones! What magnificent buildings!"
>
> "Do you see all these great buildings?" replied Jesus. "Not one stone here will be left on another; every one will be thrown down." (Mark 13:1–2)

Jesus is clearly not impressed.

Then there was the day Jesus turned over the money changers' tables in the temple courts. Upon being asked for a sign of his authority to do such things, Jesus said this:

> Jesus answered them, "Destroy this temple, and I will raise it again in three days."
>
> They replied, "It has taken forty-six years to build this temple, and you are going to raise it in three days?" But the temple he had spoken of was his body. (John 2:19–21)

This is Jesus Messiah, the Living Stone, the one rejected by the build-ers, crucified, and raised from the dead. He is the Chief Cornerstone.

The cornerstone is the first stone laid in the foundation, and it becomes the singular point of reference for every other stone.

I am tempted to ask the question, "Is Jesus your Cornerstone?" but it is a ridiculous question. It would be like asking, "Is the sun your sun?" It is *the* sun. The question is, "Am I referencing my entire life around the Cornerstone?" Because if I'm not, I am stumbling and falling and ultimately failing.

I am also tempted to ask the question, "Are you building your life on the Cornerstone?" which is also the wrong question. The truth? If I have come to the Living Stone, the one the builders rejected, the one who has become the Chief Cornerstone, I am no longer building my life. He is the builder. I am, according to the text, "being built into a spiritual house to be a holy priesthood, offering spiritual sacrifices acceptable to God through Jesus Christ" (1 Peter 2:5).

Jesus Messiah is building his church, and as I come to him, the Living Stone, he incorporates me as a living stone into his building project, the church, the only entity on earth against which the gates of hell will never prevail. It's why we sing, "My hope is built on nothing less than Jesus' blood and righteousness; I dare not trust the sweetest frame, but wholly lean on Jesus' name."[1]

The Prayer

Jesus, you are the Messiah, the Son of the living God. You are the stone the builders rejected, who has become the Chief Cornerstone. Thank you for the grace of calling us to lay down the building project formerly known as our lives, and then for building us into the realm and reality you call "my church." We confess that we do not build our lives. You are the builder. We are being built by you. Holy Spirit, increase our awareness of this truth until it is our experienced reality. Praying in Jesus' name. Amen.

The Questions

Why do people reject Jesus? (The answer can't be "the church" because there was no church when people first rejected him. They still reject him now for the same reason they rejected him then.)

---

1. Edward Mote, "My Hope Is Built on Nothing Less" (1834). Public domain.

Week 2:
Discussion Questions

Hearing the Text: 1 Peter 1:13–2:8

Therefore, with minds that are alert and fully sober, set your hope on the grace to be brought to you when Jesus Christ is revealed at his coming. As obedient children, do not conform to the evil desires you had when you lived in ignorance. But just as he who called you is holy, so be holy in all you do; for it is written: "Be holy, because I am holy."

Since you call on a Father who judges each person's work impartially, live out your time as foreigners here in reverent fear. For you know that it was not with perishable things such as silver or gold that you were redeemed from the empty way of life handed down to you from your ancestors, but with the precious blood of Christ, a lamb without blemish or defect. He was chosen before the creation of the world, but was revealed in these last times for your sake. Through him you believe in God, who raised him from the dead and glorified him, and so your faith and hope are in God.

Now that you have purified yourselves by obeying the truth so that you have sincere love for each other, love one another deeply, from the heart. For you have been born again, not of perishable seed, but of imperishable, through the living and enduring word of God. For,

> "All people are like grass,
> and all their glory is like the flowers of the field;
> the grass withers and the flowers fall,
> but the word of the Lord endures forever."

And this is the word that was preached to you.

Therefore, rid yourselves of all malice and all deceit, hypocrisy, envy, and slander of every kind. Like newborn babies, crave pure spiritual milk, so that by it you may grow up in your salvation, now that you have tasted that the Lord is good.

As you come to him, the living Stone—rejected by humans but chosen by God and precious to him—you also, like living stones, are being built into a spiritual house to be a holy priesthood, offering spiritual sacrifices acceptable to God through Jesus Christ. For in Scripture it says:

> *"See, I lay a stone in Zion,*
> *a chosen and precious cornerstone,*
> *and the one who trusts in him*
> *will never be put to shame."*

Now to you who believe, this stone is precious. But to those who do not believe,

> *"The stone the builders rejected*
> *has become the cornerstone,"*

and,

> *"A stone that causes people to stumble*
> *and a rock that makes them fall."*

They stumble because they disobey the message—which is also what they were destined for.

Responding to the Text

- What did you hear?
- What did you see?
- What did you otherwise sense from the Lord?

Sharing Insights and Implications for Discipleship

Drawing from the Scripture text and daily readings, what did you find challenging, encouraging, provocative, comforting, invasive, inspiring, corrective, affirming, guiding, or warning?

Shaping Intentions for Prayer

Write your discipleship intention for the week ahead.

3
WEEK

---

1 Peter 2:9–10

---

1 Peter 2:9–10

15

The Church Jesus Is Building: A Chosen People

> But you are a chosen people, a royal priesthood, a holy nation, God's special possession, that you may declare the praises of him who called you out of darkness into his wonderful light. Once you were not a people, but now you are the people of God; once you had not received mercy, but now you have received mercy.

===== **Consider This** =====

In C. S. Lewis's *The Screwtape Letters*, a senior demon named Screwtape describes the church as "one of our great allies" that is "quite invisible."[1] I never thought I'd find myself agreeing with a demon. While I believe more than ever in the church Jesus is building, it remains "quite invisible" (at least to me). I don't think I have ever seen it—at least not as Peter describes it. Why do I say this?

Look around.

We find ourselves at a moment in history that calls for excessive humility and extreme honesty. It is a moment not for hand-wringing anxiety but for peace-filled desperation. We have been through long cycles of evolution and devolution, of layering on sociological theory, heretical teaching, and worldly growth principles. It seems time now for a massive yard sale.

We can and must return to the Lord with all our hearts, for only Jesus can restore us to the church of his making. That's the church we all long to see and be part of. Peter describes it in four parts: as (1) a chosen people, (2) a royal priesthood, (3) a holy nation, and (4) God's special possession.

We will make camp in 1 Peter 2:9–10 for the next several chapters,

---

1. C. S. Lewis, *The Screwtape Letters* (1942; repr., San Francisco: HarperSanFrancisco, 2001), 5.

examining each of these aspects Peter describes. My hope is that, rather than ranting, we will seek restoration to our deepest identity and vocation.

To that end, let's consider more closely the first descriptor Peter offers: *a chosen people.*

According to the revealed Word of God, at the center of all that is and was and ever shall be, seen and unseen, is the embodied person, visible and incarnate in glorified human flesh, the resurrected, ascended Savior—the Lord of heaven and earth—Jesus Messiah.

Go back and read that sentence again very slowly. If we cannot begin here, with this revealed reality, we cannot begin at all.

We are a chosen people only because, and to the extent that, we have chosen to follow this person, Jesus Messiah—period, full stop. This is to say we have surrendered our broken past to him, entrusted our eternal destiny to him, and pledged our ever-present love and loyalty to him. Because he is at the center of all that is real and because by the grace and mercy of God this truth has been revealed to us, we have chosen to join the glad procession of people on a pilgrimage to meet him face-to-face. This is what it means to be "a chosen people." And the mystery of the gospel is that though we are on our way to meet him, he is with us every step of the way. It's why Peter said this:

> Though you have not seen him, you love him; and even though you do not see him now, you believe in him and are filled with an inexpressible and glorious joy, for you are receiving the end result of your faith, the salvation of your souls. (1 Peter 1:8–9)

The Christian faith is not an ethereal, fluffy philosophy. It is the concretized, mystical union between Jesus Christ and his people. We grasp the true meaning of our chosenness when we wake up to the fact that God chose us, and then in response, we reorient our entire lives around seeking him and his kingdom.

The big question we must reckon with is this one: Will we understand the church Jesus is building—a chosen people—as a centered set or a bounded set? In other words, will we focus our attention on the center or the circumference? There is a great deal of fear and anxiety around determining the circumference. We fear if we don't nail down the boundaries, we will lose the center altogether. The opposite is true. If we don't fix our gaze on the ever-clear and clarifying center of Jesus Messiah and his kingdom, all boundaries will become confused and irrelevant and will ultimately distract people from the central pursuit.

Will we focus our energy on a shared pursuit of our common center, or will we fix our attention on the circumference, defining the boundaries of who is in and who is out? Far from arguing for some kind of fuzzy universalism, we are calling for a crystallized Christocentrism (aka Christ-centeredness). After all, didn't Jesus say, "And I, when I am lifted up from the earth, will draw all people to myself" (John 12:32)?

It is time for the chosen people to give everything they have to lifting up the one who chose them. Here's the secret. If you clarify the center, the center will gently and graciously form the circumference. The conversation will cease to be about who is in the circle and who is outside of it, and instead will become about who is moving toward the center and who is moving away from it—and how to encourage and embrace both. This naturally raises the whole point of the next mark of the church Jesus is building—a royal priesthood.

I believe the witness of the Scriptures and the Spirit is that the church Jesus is building is not a bounded set but a centered set. This is, at least in part, how I understand this mark of the church as "a chosen people." Does this mean everyone will wind up in the church Jesus is building? Likely not, but it's time to stop asking that question. It's the wrong question. The question that pleases Jesus is this one: How might everyone in my sphere of life and influence find and be found by Jesus? And, of course, this has no hope of happening through my agency unless Jesus becomes the defining center of my life.

The Prayer

Jesus, you are the Messiah, the Son of the living God. Thank you for choosing us. Thank you for choosing me. Thank you for the grace you keep giving to help us choose you continually, come what may. Be lifted up today in our hearts, our homes, our churches, and, yes, our towns and cities. Our greatest concern is that everyone come to the place of choosing you, which is to know they have been chosen by you. Could that begin with us letting them know that we choose them too? Holy Spirit, endue us with this grace of choosing others before they choose us. Praying in Jesus' name. Amen.

═══ The Questions ═══

What is it about us that fixates on drawing boundary lines, defining the insiders and the outsiders, and otherwise policing the circumference? What would it mean to become fixated on the center instead? What might happen? What might not happen?

16

1 Peter 2:9–10

The Church Jesus Is Building: A Royal Priesthood

> *But you are a chosen people, a royal priesthood, a holy nation, God's special possession, that you may declare the praises of him who called you out of darkness into his wonderful light. Once you were not a people, but now you are the people of God; once you had not received mercy, but now you have received mercy.*

═══ Consider This ═══

If we are making the shift from the bounded-set approach to the church Jesus is building (which I don't believe is the church he is building) to the centered-set approach, it means we switch from policing the boundaries to blazing paths toward the center. This is priestly work. It's why the path moves from a chosen people to a royal priesthood.

For starters, what is a priest? My simplest definition would be a person acting with agency and authority who represents God to people and people to God—working to embody and effect an exchange of life, light, and love between them. I love the way Dan Wilt said it in his Daily Text series on the Holy Spirit. I want you to relish every word of this:

In the Biblical ideal, a "priest" is a holy, set-apart one, a true meeting place of heaven and earth, an image-bearing, human sanctuary who embodies unbroken worship and unceasing covenant loyalty. A priest is to be one who, anointed by the Spirit, nurtures and facilitates the connection between God and people. A priest is to take another's hand to guide the way to wholeness in relationship with God. A priest is to lead a heart to embrace God's great story of rescue and restoration—with all its personal and corporate implications. A priest is one who calls God's people to worship in spirit and in truth, to maintain covenant love, and to thereby resist idolatry—and the injustice, dehumanization, and spiritual disorientation that inevitably follow it.[2]

In short, a royal priest moves about among the human race, helping to orient people with the King who sits on the throne at the center of it all. These priests don't wear robes and collars; they wear ordinary clothes. In fact, they wear what you are wearing right now. How do I know? Because these priests are you, dear friend. I am describing you.

Wait, you might be thinking, *I'm not a priest. I'm just a layperson!*

Please, please, please banish this phrase "just a layperson" from your speech.

Let me use an analogy here. Imagine your favorite athlete was being interviewed before their next big game and responded to a question about the sport by saying, "Well, I'm just a player." It would be absurd, wouldn't it?

It's the same thing when a person says, "I'm just a layperson." They're implying that the pastors, priests, or professional ministry staff are the real players when, in fact, those people hold the role of coaches.

This is the absurdity of the moment we find ourselves stuck in. The coaches are on the field, and the players are in the stands.

You are a living signpost pointing people to our King and good Father and helping them get there. To hold your hand is to feel the

---

2. Dan Wilt, *Receive the Holy Spirit: A 70-Day Journey Through the Scriptures* (Franklin, TN: Seedbed, 2022), 68.

clasp of mercy. To listen to your voice is to hear the sound of grace. To be in your presence is to smell the fragrance of Christ. To behold your countenance is to share in the very peace of Jesus. To sit with you at table is to taste and see that the Lord is good. You, priest, are a living reminder of the love of God, a wayfinder for the lost, and a waymaker for the weary. Instead of giving directions, you walk with them along the road. At times, you will seem to follow their lead in the wrong direction, patiently waiting for them to come to the end of their broken self and make the turn toward home. At other times, you will stand at the end of the road, seeing beyond its winding ways, with your eyes peeled on the horizon as you look for the fragile frames of returning sons and daughters—ready to run at the drop of a hat.

This is what a royal priesthood looks like. This is how it works. This is what it does. Everyone is called. Everyone is a priest.

So now you know. You have a job to do all day long—today and tomorrow and the next day. It is simple and yet challenging. You are a royal priest. I'm thinking of starting a school for royal priests. But wait! Hang on. That's already been done. It's called the church Jesus is building!

The Prayer

Jesus, you are the Messiah, the Son of the living God. Thank you for calling every single one of us. Thank you for anointing every single one of us as a royal priest. Make us into your royal priests. That is our ambition, Jesus, to represent you to people, and people to you. We want to be all those things that fit the description of royal priests. Something tells me if we keep our eyes fixed on you, the Holy Spirit will shape us to become like you. We want to be a meeting place of heaven and earth. Praying in Jesus' name. Amen.

The Questions

Do you think of yourself as a priest? How about a royal priest? Why or why not? Are you inspired to live into this reality? What holds you back?

17

1 Peter 2:9-10

The Church Jesus Is Building: A Holy Nation

> But you are a chosen people, a royal priesthood, a holy nation, God's special possession, that you may declare the praises of him who called you out of darkness into his wonderful light. Once you were not a people, but now you are the people of God; once you had not received mercy, but now you have received mercy.

===== **Consider This** =====

Today we come to a third major feature of the church Jesus is building—a holy nation. Before we talk about its meaning, let's talk about what it does not mean. The whole concept of *nation* has come to mean many things over the years. For starters, and most readily, it means a geopolitical territory marked by land and borders. The "holy nation" Peter refers to is not a geopolitical territory marked by land and borders.

The term *nation* has also come to represent any grouping of people who are held together by some kind of tribal loyalty or affiliation. Most every university with a football team now refers to itself as Hog Nation or Gator Nation and so forth. I have even found myself referring to Seedbed Daily Text subscribers as Sower Nation on occasion. This concept of nation loosely translates to the notion of a tribe. That's closer to what Peter means, but it's still a miss.

The church Jesus is building is a holy nation that transcends any and every national border, and it blows tribes and tribalism out of the water. The term Peter used for the English term *nation* is *ethnos*. It means a distinct people group. So if this nation's distinctiveness is not based on nationality, ethnicity, tribal loyalty, culture, language, family of origin, or any of the other usual markers of identity, what makes it identifiable and distinctive? That is the question, isn't it?

You are a . . . holy nation.

Let's remember how Peter opened this letter.

> To God's elect, exiles scattered throughout the provinces of Pontus, Galatia, Cappadocia, Asia and Bithynia, who have been chosen according to the foreknowledge of God the Father, through the sanctifying work of the Spirit, to be obedient to Jesus Christ and sprinkled with his blood. (1 Peter 1:1–2)

Exiles. Scattered. These are the two main things that would seem to go against nationhood. Add that to the geographical dispersion (or diaspora) of all the places Peter names. What do these people even have in common? They don't even know each other.

We know that Peter has written, "You are a . . . holy nation." So is it their holiness that unites them? This is where the church goes south. This is where we get back to the bounded set, because holiness quickly reverts to behavior and image management and who is in and who is out, and the circle keeps getting smaller and smaller until it's just a few Pharisees holding a rule book in the end. It's not the rules that these scattered exiles have in common; it's the Ruler. In the New Testament, *holy* means one thing and one thing only—Jesus.

It's all Peter can talk about. By my count, he references Jesus no fewer than thirty-eight times in the five short chapters of his letter. Here's what Peter wants us to know: holiness is a person. When he writes, "Be holy, because I am holy," Peter knows the "I am" is Jesus. He knows the only way to be holy, as Jesus is holy, is to be filled with the Spirit of Jesus, who is the Spirit of holiness.

And one more thing Peter knows: he knows that the holiness of Jesus is a contagious holiness. In the old understanding, if something or someone unholy touched a holy thing or person, the holy person or object became unholy. With Jesus, it is just the opposite. Everything and everyone the Holy One touches—no matter their condition— becomes holy.

Jesus people of the world, unite. You are a chosen people, a royal priesthood, a holy nation—indeed, God's special possession.

Jesus, you are the Messiah, the Son of the living God. You are not only holy; you are the very holy of holies, the most holy place. You are the resplendent holiness of God who makes the unclean clean, who makes the unholy holy, who causes the blind to see, the lame to walk, even the dead to rise. We would exchange our idea of holy for your vision of holiness. We want you, Jesus. We want to be part of the holy nation. Come, Holy Spirit, and make it so. Praying in Jesus' name. Amen.

The Questions

Doesn't it strike you as so much easier and infinitely more refreshing to fix your eyes on Jesus, to lift your heart to Jesus, to set your mind on Jesus, to offer your body to Jesus, than to focus on whether you are being holy enough? In what ways have you been striving for holiness? How can you remember that holiness is the fruit of the Spirit's presence in you?

18

1 Peter 2:9–10

The Church Jesus Is Building: God's Special Possession

> But you are a chosen people, a royal priesthood, a holy nation, God's special possession, that you may declare the praises of him who called you out of darkness into his wonderful light. Once you were not a people, but now you are the people of God; once you had not received mercy, but now you have received mercy.

Consider This

God loves all people, but he especially loves his own people. He calls us—the church Jesus is building—his "special possession." It's the same for us, isn't it? We love all people, or we want to, but we especially love our own people. We love other people's children, but somehow we love our own children more. They are our "special possession." This is where God takes it to the next level. The living God loves all people so much that he wants *all of them* to become his own children, his special possession. How do we know this? Because he sent his Son, Jesus Messiah, to reveal the depths of his love for us—to rescue us, to redeem us, and to make us his own very special possession. Read this text in that light.

> He came to that which was his own, but his own did not receive him. Yet to all who did receive him, to those who believed in his name, he gave the right to become children of God— children born not of natural descent, nor of human decision or a husband's will, but born of God. (John 1:11–13)

The amazing thing about our God is the way his love and posture toward us are all at once so extravagant as to be an exclusive kind of love and also radically inclusive in their reach. In other words, the grace of God in Jesus Christ is available only to those who will receive it, and yet everyone is a qualified candidate to receive it. Everyone is preapproved, but you have to accept the offer if you would be born of God and become his special possession.

People balk at the notion that the only way to know this God is through Jesus Christ—as though that were somehow unfair or unjust. Imagine you wanted to give me a million dollars. You have the check made out to me. You only ask that I come to your house so you can get to know me and I can get to know you. The money cannot be mailed or transferred in any other way. Would that be unfair or unjust? There would be only one way to get it. Or take it out of the financial realm and put it in the medical field. You have the one cure for the disease I suffer with, and without the cure I will die. All I need to do is come to you to receive it. Upon receiving the cure, I would become part of one of the most extraordinary groups of people in the world. Wouldn't I want this?

Isn't that what Peter is trying to convey when he says what all of this is for?

> . . . that you may declare the praises of him who called you

out of darkness into his wonderful light. Once you were not a people, but now you are the people of God; once you had not received mercy, but now you have received mercy.

The church Jesus is building is God's special possession. And there is room for the whole world. No one is excluded unless they exclude themselves, unless they choose not to receive the offer and the opportunity.

Who wouldn't want to become the special possession of the God of heaven and earth? Who wouldn't want to be part of a people who have walked out of darkness and into marvelous light? Who wouldn't want to be part of a people who have received the extraordinary mercy of Jesus Messiah?

This is the church Jesus is building. I'm looking for this church, and something tells me you are too; even as we are a part of it, we are looking for it.

═══ The Prayer ═══

Jesus, you are the Messiah, the Son of the living God. What a fellowship, to be part of a people who are your chosen people, a royal priesthood, a holy nation, and your special possession. This is so extraordinary. Forgive us for the hundreds of times we have just read right past all of this exceedingly extravagant truth. Would you lead us deeper into the experience of these realities? Would you grant us the humility to enter into such a group of people? We confess that we can find so much wrong with so many churches and so many people, and yet you are at work in them. Holy Spirit, open our eyes. Lead us by faith. Let the miracle begin with us. Praying in Jesus' name. Amen.

═══ The Questions ═══

God's special possession—does it hit you differently this time? Or not so much? You are defined as such a person. How does this understanding affect your forward progress? Does it make you want to share with others your experience of this reality in new and fresh ways?

1 Peter 2:9–10

19 Have You Received Mercy?

> But you are a chosen people, a royal priesthood, a holy nation, God's special possession, that you may declare the praises of him who called you out of darkness into his wonderful light. Once you were not a people, but now you are the people of God; once you had not received mercy, but now you have received mercy.

═══ Consider This ═══

The church Peter is speaking to here includes little collections and constellations of people who have responded to the call of Jesus to come out of darkness and into his wonderful light. They are little collections of persons who were once "not a people" and who have now become "the people of God." They are little collections of persons who have "received mercy."

I have been in many churches filled with wonderfully self-sufficient, independent people. They are part of the church like they are part of the Rotary or the Lions Club. They are upstanding and often outstanding citizens—good people. They are missing one critical thing. They have not received mercy. And they have not received mercy because they have never known their need for mercy.

These kinds of folks have understood the people Peter speaks of here as those who have made mistakes, often big mistakes; their life choices have led them to places of darkness and obvious desperation, where they needed rescue and mercy and, yes, salvation. Our churches are also filled with many more people who have accepted the "terms of salvation" on the basis of a doctrinal understanding; they legitimately understand themselves as "Christians," and yet they have not "received mercy."

People who have "received mercy" are sometimes people who came to the end of their rope, and yet many more did not. They simply came to a providential awakening to their need of God. I'm not talking about their need for God to solve some problem for them (though that may have contributed), but about their need for God at the core of their being. Often this means coming to terms with the thing that promised them mercy but never quite delivered. Anyone who has received mercy knows that they know they were made for God and that without God they will perish, even if they go on living.

People who have received mercy know that they know they simply cannot function without Jesus, who is the mercy of God. They know it, not theoretically, but experientially. They do not judge others, because they know that there but for the mercy of God go they. Herein lives "church."

Whenever and wherever and however these people find each other and make themselves at home in the spacious communion of Father, Son, and Holy Spirit, you have church. This is why you can have church at work, in prison, at a recovery meeting, at school, in an emergency shelter filled with refugees, or in a hospital waiting room. And this is why you may not actually have "church" in the building on the corner we call "our church."

Church turns out to be the ones who have received mercy—those who bow down together as the chosen people, the royal priesthood, the holy nation, indeed God's special possession. They are the ones who are declaring the praises of him who called us out of darkness and into his marvelous light. These people aren't better than anyone else. They are just a whole lot humbler and more loving and, yes, more merciful. You know them when you see them. So at all costs, the invitation is to find church—to band together with these people who have received mercy and become one of them, and then to plant "church" everywhere you go.

The Prayer

Jesus, you are the Messiah, the Son of the living God. We desperately long for the church you are building. Thank you for bringing us "church," for making us "church," and for planting "church" through our simply being together and united in you. Forgive us for the ways we have missed it and messed it up. Thank you for the mercy of endless do-overs. Holy Spirit, stir up in me the deepest core longing to receive mercy. Even if I have already received mercy, stir it up even deeper. Praying in Jesus' name. Amen.

Have you "received mercy"? Do you know that you know? Don't be afraid to be honest. Jesus relates to who we are and where we are. He's often simply looking for the straightforward humility of honesty. I sense awakening is afoot in so many people these days. And it doesn't mean discounting what has gone before. It all counts.

---

1 Peter 2:9–10

The Praying Church

20

> But you are a chosen people, a royal priesthood, a holy nation, God's special possession, that you may declare the praises of him who called you out of darkness into his wonderful light. Once you were not a people, but now you are the people of God; once you had not received mercy, but now you have received mercy.

===== **Consider This** =====

We believe the church of Jesus Christ is the dwelling place of Almighty God on planet Earth.

Therefore, all we believe to be true about the living God, we believe to be true about his people.

If the holy love, power, and presence of God are dwelling within God's chosen people, God's royal priesthood, God's holy nation, God's special possession, it means at least two things: (1) we have been granted extraordinary authority, and (2) we possess enormous responsibility. Think of it as response-ability. We have the authority and responsibility to respond in a way no other organization or institution on planet Earth possesses.

We desperately need to grasp the real facts on the ground, not as reported by the news media but as informed by the revelation of the Word and Spirit, and to understand the rules of engagement. Given all we are exploring about the nature of the church Jesus is building, here are the facts on the ground:

1. The body of Christ is a global fellowship bonded together by the Holy Spirit. Remember, we are living stones being built together into a spiritual house. Our connection is not institutional in nature, but supernatural. We are quite literally part of each other—connected like a hand is to an arm. This has enormous implications for the church in regions where conflict continues without any end in sight (the conflict between Ukraine and Russia was on my mind when writing this book): "If one part suffers, every part suffers with it; if one part is honored, every part rejoices with it" (1 Corinthians 12:26).

2. Jesus Christ is the head of the body—the Lord of heaven and earth, resurrected and ascended, living and active, speaking and listening, guiding and directing. He leads the intercession of the church. We must lift our hearts to Jesus, set our minds on Jesus, fix our eyes on Jesus, and offer our bodies to Jesus. He is the commander of angel armies and Lord of the church.

3. The Holy Spirit is the Spirit of prayer who is praying without ceasing in words and in groans too deep for words. As we invite the Spirit to fill us with his own prayers, we will begin to sense the agony in this world, and our hearts will begin to attune to the Spirit's praying. Prayer is not something we initiate; prayer is the initiative of the Holy Spirit. We do not initiate; we participate. Prayer is not ginning up more spiritual activity; prayer is getting low to the ground and cultivating receptivity.

We must pray. And I'm not talking about prayer as the "when all else fails, do this" sentiment we see written on placards and Instagram posts every time something bad happens in the world. I am talking about prayer as battle strategy. Prayer as war. The call to prayer is not a call to "say prayers" and then move on. Prayer is the call to a deep awareness of the presence of God; a surrendered attention to the Lord of the church, Jesus Christ; a keen attunement to the voice of the Spirit; and a bonded attachment to one another across the body of Christ. The call to prayer is the urgent admonition to lay aside the religious customs of casual prayer and enter into the zone of the kingdom of heaven, abiding together in the presence and person of Jesus Messiah for the sake of the world.

There is a common and almost prevailing mentality around prayer that centers its authority in its sincerity, fervency, and collectivist spirit (How many people can we get to join in?). This feels to me like religious activism, like a spiritual protest movement. If we can just get God's attention, giving ourselves no rest and giving God no rest (marshaling the precedent of Isaiah 62:6–7), God will be forced to act. Though this approach has a seductive allure to it, it just doesn't strike me as the approach taken by the New Testament people of God. The New Testament vision of prayer at the center of the church Jesus is building looks like transcendent activity. It is the presence and power of God moving in lockstep with a community of people. Examine how Paul instructs the church concerning prayer:

> Finally, be strong in the Lord and in his mighty power. Put on the full armor of God, so that you can take your stand against the devil's schemes. For our struggle is not against flesh and blood, but against the rulers, against the authorities, against the powers of this dark world and against the spiritual forces of evil in the heavenly realms. (Ephesians 6:10–12)

What are the implications of this text?

1. Prayer does not begin with a people in one place crying out to a God who is somewhere else, hoping God will do something in yet another place. Prayer is an active, direct, warlike engagement.
2. Prayer begins not with people but with God. Prayer is the initiative of God to share the burden of his love for the world with his image bearers—namely, us—and prayer is the Spirit-infused responsiveness of God's people to share in and supernaturally carry this burden to the point where his kingdom manifests itself on earth as it is in heaven (that is, blind see, deaf hear, lame walk, lepers are cleansed, dead are raised, poor hear good news).
3. In prayer, we always come up against the kingdom of darkness

and death, making prayer a very dangerous activity. In prayer, we are engaging with powers, authorities, rulers, and principalities—indeed the realms of darkness and evil—against which we are no match. Hence, we are instructed to "put on the full armor of God."

4. Prayer is the mysterious and holy union of God with his people in a divine-human collaborative agency, inextricably bound together in an abiding fellowship coursing with an uncontainable strength and mighty power. Remember, the leader of this movement, the head of the church (not to mention the victorious Lord of heaven and earth), is fully God and fully human.

Church, the time for casual prayer has passed. The age of prayer as "last resort" is over. The practice of prayer as expressing our anxieties is done. We are waking up to the sobering presence of Jesus Christ as our Great High Priest. We are beginning to sense the desperation of the Holy Spirit, who travails for the deliverance of the whole earth from the rogue and defeated powers of sin and death.

Prayer is not, nor can it ever be, reduced to religious or even spiritual activism. It is instead the transcendent activity of God in the midst of the church Jesus is building for the sake of the world. Church, let us pray.

The Prayer

Jesus, you are the Messiah, the Son of the living God. We desperately long for the church you are building. Holy Spirit, would you lead us onto this holy ground and into this sacred assembly? Praying in Jesus' name. Amen.

The Questions

I hope you are not hearing these writings as being critical of our local churches or especially our leaders. There is no time for that kind of navel-gazing. This is much deeper than that. I wonder if you are sensing a deepened longing in your spirit these days. Are you getting in touch with the desperation of the world for God? These are the birth pangs of awakening. Let's stay with them.

Week 3:
Discussion Questions

Hearing the Text: 1 Peter 2:9–10

But you are a chosen people, a royal priesthood, a holy nation, God's special possession, that you may declare the praises of him who called you out of darkness into his wonderful light. Once you were not a people, but now you are the people of God; once you had not received mercy, but now you have received mercy.

Responding to the Text

- What did you hear?
- What did you see?
- What did you otherwise sense from the Lord?

Sharing Insights and Implications for Discipleship

Drawing from the Scripture text and daily readings, what did you find challenging, encouraging, provocative, comforting, invasive, inspiring, corrective, affirming, guiding, or warning?

Shaping Intentions for Prayer

Write your discipleship intention for the week ahead.

4
WEEK

---

1 Peter 2:11–3:6

22

1 Peter 2:11

Outside-In to Inside-Out Transformation

> *Dear friends, I urge you, as foreigners and exiles, to abstain from sinful desires, which wage war against your soul.*

===== **Consider This** =====

Sin is not fundamentally a behavioral problem. It is much deeper than this. Peter is not telling these followers of Jesus to behave. He's talking about *desire*. That's the real battlefield, isn't it?

Our desires drag us away. Desire conceives and gives birth to sin. Sin grows up, and when it does, it gives birth to death. James puts it this way:

> When tempted, no one should say, "God is tempting me." For God cannot be tempted by evil, nor does he tempt anyone; but each person is tempted when they are dragged away by their own evil desire and enticed. Then, after desire has conceived, it gives birth to sin; and sin, when it is full-grown, gives birth to death. (James 1:13–15)

It is very urgent. I mean, how long has anger been growing in your life? How about jealousy or envy? How about lust? How about slander and gossip? Aren't you ready to get out of the cesspool of feeling better about yourself because you have learned to feel bad about yourself (i.e., bondage to guilt and shame)?

Yet behavior management is a lost cause. If whatever we struggle with gets to the level of our behavior, we have already lost. Any apostle worth their salt knows the futility of trying to manage one's behavior—especially Peter. Remember that time Jesus called him Satan? Or how about the time he cut off a guy's ear? By nature, Peter was impulsive. He tended to say what he thought before he even thought it. Let's remember, Peter was there when Jesus said this:

You have heard that it was said to the people long ago, "You shall not murder, and anyone who murders will be subject to judgment." But I tell you that anyone who is angry with a brother or sister will be subject to judgment. . . . You have heard that it was said, "You shall not commit adultery." But I tell you that anyone who looks at a woman lustfully has already committed adultery with her in his heart. (Matthew 5:21–22, 27–28)

Jesus teaches us that sinful actions don't begin with behavioral actions; they begin in the heart of a person. I believe this is the locus of what I call the "Three Musketeers of the Soul"—our affections, dispositions, and desires.

We are so stuck at the surface, trying to discipline our behavior, when all the while, the real work is in the deeper places—the transformation of our affections, dispositions, and desires. Outside-in approaches just don't work. It's why Jesus goes for the inside-out approach. While law, and consequently legalism, works at the level of behavior and action, the love of God in Jesus Christ works at the level of the heart.

Now imagine if desire could be harnessed in the other direction. That is the good news. By his indwelling presence in us, Jesus reverses the curse of sinful desires, turning them into the desires of the heart. This is where the other two musketeers—our affections and dispositions—come into play.

When our affections are oriented around God, our dispositions begin to change toward ourselves and others. In this process, our formerly sinful desires become displaced by the Holy Spirit–given desires of our hearts. We then learn to operate out of our new creation self, trusting our desires and living from them, freely and fully alive, because they are God-given—whole and holy.

═══ The Prayer ═══

Jesus, you are the Messiah, the Son of the living God. Thank you for the amazing way you take my broken self and sinful desires and put me back together in complete wholeness, integrity, and love. Sort out my affections, dispositions, and desires. I give you my broken desires and would receive from you the restored desires of my heart. Fill me with your Spirit in such a way that my old and broken dispositions become displaced by the disposition of the love of Jesus. And then kindle desire in me to love what you love, even myself and or especially myself. Lead me into this mystery. Holy Spirit; lead me in this path. I am weary of the internal struggle. Praying in Jesus' name. Amen.

═══ The Questions ═══

How are you processing this connection between affections, dispositions, and desires as opposed to fighting and managing behavior patterns? How have you seen this inside-out process working in your own life? How has the outside-in approach worked for you? Affections, dispositions, and desires—does this inside-out connection ring true?

23

1 Peter 2:12

Such Good Lives . . .

> *Live such good lives among the pagans that, though they accuse you of doing wrong, they may see your good deeds and glorify God on the day he visits us.*

═══ Consider This ═══

It is truly unfathomable to consider all that Peter has covered so far with such an economy of words. As we are learning to read the Bible better, it is important to always keep the context around us. I encourage you to read the whole letter at least once a week during our journey, if not every day. The more you cover it, the more it will cover you.

Remember how Peter opened the letter? "To God's elect, exiles scattered throughout the provinces of Pontus, Galatia, Cappadocia, Asia and Bithynia . . ." (1 Peter 1:1). Look where he is in 1 Peter 2:11, the verse before today's text: "Dear friends, I urge you, as foreigners and exiles . . ."

Peter reminds them of their context and even more of their identity. He says in essence, "You have a home there, but there is not your home. You are a foreigner." He would say to us, "You are a resident of the United States (or Russia or Ukraine or insert your own country here), but you are a citizen of the kingdom of heaven."

For the rest of chapter 1, Peter talks about his favorite subject—our King, Jesus Messiah—and orients us with our identity in him and sets the stage for the future. He opens chapter 2 by encouraging us to wean off the "chips and salsa" diet and to "crave pure spiritual milk, so that by it you may grow up in your salvation" (verse 2).

Then he reveals to us what we are a part of—the church Jesus is building. He gives us the charter: (1) chosen people, (2) royal priesthood, (3) holy nation, and (4) God's special possession. This is not a "your best life now" spiritual self-improvement program. This is "the Church as we see her spread out through all time and space and rooted in eternity, terrible as an army with banners,"[1] to quote C. S. Lewis, and the victory is won through the testimony of many witnesses who have received mercy and become not just new persons but a completely new kind of people together.

Now Peter turns to the matter of character, but he doesn't address it at the level of behavior management. He's dealing at the desire and soul level, as if to say the only way to win the war "out there" is to win the battles "in here." Peter is looking not for legalistic rule followers but for souls made of gold and people who are living such good lives that gladness wells up in unbelievers around them. Peter is looking for deeds of pure goodness, inexplicable kindness—deeds that are ordinary on one level and yet carry something of our home country in them, deeds that are weighted with the very goodness of our King and his kingdom. Because, remember, we are "foreigners and exiles" here. Peter is looking for deeds that inspire the worship of our God—King Jesus—by the very people who have been led to despise us by the false narratives of the empire.

---

1. Lewis, *Screwtape Letters*, 5.

Jesus, you are the Messiah, the Son of the living God. We want to live such good lives that people are drawn to Jesus. We want to live such lives of hospitality, kindness, goodness, and generosity that people come to be in awe of God. Holy Spirit, displace the self-rule in us with the rule of the King. Fill us with the love of God that we have strangely forgotten. We want the disposition of Jesus, that our affections might be anchored in you, that our desires might be for the kingdom. Praying in Jesus' name. Amen.

The Questions

What's your main takeaway from the journey so far in 1 Peter?

24

1 Peter 2:13–17

Submission versus Obedience

> *Submit yourselves for the Lord's sake to every human authority: whether to the emperor, as the supreme authority, or to governors, who are sent by him to punish those who do wrong and to commend those who do right. For it is God's will that by doing good you should silence the ignorant talk of foolish people. Live as free people, but do not use your freedom as a cover-up for evil; live as God's slaves. Show proper respect to everyone, love the family of believers, fear God, honor the emperor.*

Consider This

Government matters—a lot. God created government. This is why we as the followers of Jesus, as his church, must have a very clear, clean, and unconventionally humble relationship with the state. The question for all of us is, How do we do this?

> Submit yourselves for the Lord's sake to every human authority . . .

As an American, I find that something in me wants to thwart, rebel against, and otherwise resist the authority of the government, especially if I disagree with their decisions or rationales (which I admittedly increasingly question and doubt). But as a Christian I have to honestly reckon with the Word of God that charges us to submit to every human authority for the sake of the Lord.

Here's the kicker. Peter (and in other places Paul and even Jesus) was not writing to twenty-first-century Americans who live in a federal, constitutional, representative, democratic republic. No, he was speaking directly into a context where the government was headed by despotic, dictatorial leaders who were actively and often ruthlessly oppressing believers. In other words, Peter didn't have the likes of Joe Biden or Donald Trump in mind. He was thinking of a leader more like Vladimir Putin and of a government more like his nation's government. Does the name Nero ring a bell? When Peter says to honor the emperor, he is talking about Nero, one of the cruelest and most merciless, ruthless tyrants in the history of the world.

Notice Peter is not telling us to submit for our sake, to avoid hassle and trouble. He is not telling us to submit ourselves to the government for the sake of others. He is not telling us to submit ourselves to the government for the sake of the government. No, the Word of God is telling us to submit ourselves to the government for *the sake of Jesus Christ.*

As an American, I can hardly stomach the idea of submitting to a cruel, tyrannical, dictatorial leader. As a Christian, I don't see how I can avoid submitting. This clearly poses a dilemma for me and perhaps for you. This is one of those places I wish the Bible said something different. I wish Peter had inserted an "unless" in there, as in "unless the emperor goes too far and impinges on your rights to this and that and the other thing," or "unless the president is a complete reprobate or imbecile or on the wrong side of the aisle." But Peter didn't mince his words.

Notice, though, that Peter does not say to *obey* human authorities; he says to *submit* to them. Back in 1 Peter 1:22, Peter wrote this: "Now that you have purified yourselves by obeying the truth." He chose the Greek term *hypakōe* (pronounced hoop-a-**ko**-ay), which you will remember means "to hear while sitting under." This is Peter's word of choice when it comes to our response to the Word of God (aka "the truth"). Just a few chapters later, when it comes to our relationship with governing authorities, he chooses the word *hypotassō* (pronounced hoop-o-**tass**-o), which means something more like "to rank yourself under or be arranged or ordered under." The English word is *submission*. It doesn't mean obedience; it means something more like compliance. Where does compliance end and resistance begin? Here's a great example of such a scenario from the time of the exodus.

> The king of Egypt said to the Hebrew midwives, whose names were Shiphrah and Puah, "When you are helping the Hebrew women during childbirth on the delivery stool, if you see that the baby is a boy, kill him; but if it is a girl, let her live." The midwives, however, feared God and did not do what the king of Egypt had told them to do; they let the boys live. Then the king of Egypt summoned the midwives and asked them, "Why have you done this? Why have you let the boys live?"
> The midwives answered Pharaoh, "Hebrew women are not like Egyptian women; they are vigorous and give birth before the midwives arrive." (Exodus 1:15–19)

There comes a point at which submitting oneself to human authority comes at the Lord's detriment. And this is where the rub comes. What is a Christian conviction and what is an American (or insert your own nationality) value? Where is the overlap and where is the divergence? Whereas in the past we (in America) may have enjoyed more overlap, it appears in the future we will face more divergence. How shall we face it? It's why this conversation and the way we engage it are so important—from conscience to convictions to conclusions, all of it.

But the first question we must grapple with is this: Will we become the church Jesus is building, or will we become unwitting pawns of the political machinations of our time that move according to the ever-shifting spirit of the age? And to answer that one, we each must grapple with this question: Will I be a Christian American (or insert your nationality), or will I be an American Christian? Asking it another way and bringing it full circle: Is my conscience being shaped more by biblical conviction or by national values? It can be extraordinarily difficult to sort this out, because of our exceedingly high capacity for self-deception. This is why our utter and uncompromising allegiance to Jesus is the key to the kingdom of heaven and the path to true flourishing for any nation on earth.

> Submit yourselves for the Lord's sake to every human authority . . .

The Prayer

Jesus, you are the Messiah, the Son of the living God. Because you are our King and your kingdom is our home, we are exiles and foreigners here. We get this at one level, and yet we need to grasp it at all levels. Awaken us to this truth as a reality and not an ideal. We want your Word and Spirit to form our convictions and shape our conscience. Holy Spirit, would you give us the mind of Christ? Praying in Jesus' name. Amen.

The Questions

How does this framework of conscience, convictions, and conclusions help you think more clearly as a follower of Jesus? Do your loyalties and your allegiance feel more conflicted or more clarified?

25

1 Peter 2:18–20
Five Little Words Say It All

> *Slaves, in reverent fear of God submit yourselves to your masters, not only to those who are good and considerate, but also to those who are harsh. For it is commendable if someone bears up under the pain of*

> unjust suffering because they are conscious of God. But how is it to
> your credit if you receive a beating for doing wrong and endure it? But
> if you suffer for doing good and you endure it, this is commendable
> before God.

═══ Consider This ═══

It is fascinating to see where Peter takes us next. We might expect him to lay out a matrix of ifs and thens, buts and ors, unlesses and untils when it comes to submission to the governing authorities. Instead, he starts talking to the Christian slaves.

In five words, he lifts the church out of the endless questions and dilemmas about how we are to deal with human authorities. In five little words, he tells us that submitting to human authorities does not make us subject to them, because we are subject *only to God*—in fact, the only way we can live in submission to human authorities is to be subject to God alone. Did you catch those five little words in verse 18?

> Slaves, in reverent fear of God submit yourselves to your
> masters . . .

For specificity's sake, they are *in reverent fear of God*.

Wait! What? Christian slaves? Why is Peter not taking on the whole institution of slavery here? How could he stand for this? And to address it and not rebuke it seems to acquiesce in it, right?

Wrong. Peter is not somehow affirming the practice of slaveholding. Tragically, many of our forebears read this text and others like it as a way of biblically affirming the institution of slavery. Peter was dealing with the world as he found it and working within its evil constraints through a quite supernatural albeit subversive strategy to upend it.

Let's be clear though. Peter was not advocating for gradualism— that it is somehow okay to accept things as they are in light of the complexities of the world, believing that things will somehow get better slowly over time. Nor was he arguing for personalism—that evil can only be defeated person by person through individual repentance. Nor was he dealing with structuralism—this notion that sin and evil are not so much personal but structural and therefore society must be deconstructed brick by brick and reengineered in order to be somehow rid of the influences of sin and evil.

So what is Peter's quite supernatural albeit subversive strategy? The church Jesus is building—God's chosen people. A royal priesthood. A holy nation. God's special possession. There is only one strategy—the church Jesus is building, which begins, middles, and ends with absolute, adoring allegiance to Jesus Messiah.

> Slaves, in reverent fear of God submit yourselves to your masters, not only to those who are good and considerate, but also to those who are harsh.

The church Jesus is building won't be spending their time and energy wringing their hands and ranting their heads off about every little (or big) thing Fox News is against or CNN is for. The church Jesus is building left behind the Democrats and the Republicans (or insert your nation's political machinery here) a long time ago. The church Jesus is building is not living in a state of constant reactivity to the world around us, but rather "in reverent fear of God," in an ever-ready responsiveness to the revelation of Jesus Messiah, who has made us and redeemed us and who now calls and commissions us as a chosen people, a royal priesthood, a holy nation, and God's special possession.

The church Jesus is building is asking questions like these:

- How do we live together "in reverent fear of God," in radical obedience to God's Word, and in humble submission to one another?
- Where does submission to human authorities give way to the "reverent fear of God" and become grace-filled, humble resistance—even to the point of suffering and death?
- What does it look like to "suffer for doing good and endure it"?

Those five little words from today's text say it all. They say what we have lost. They say what we must find again. They say with extraordinary economy what I will spend the rest of my words for the rest of my life trying to say: *in reverent fear of God.*

The Prayer

Jesus, you are the Messiah, the Son of the living God. Thank you that not only are you God incarnate, but you walked this earth in the brilliance of a life lived in reverent fear of God. We confess to often living in a kind of casual familiarity with you. Holy Spirit, would you lead us in this way of abiding relationship with God that is marked both by intimate relationship and awe-filled reverence, by holiness and love? Praying in Jesus' name. Amen.

The Questions

What are the questions you might add to the list—the ones the church Jesus is building might be asking?

26

1 Peter 2:21–25

Why Am I Not Being Persecuted?

> *To this you were called, because Christ suffered for you, leaving you an example, that you should follow in his steps.*
> *"He committed no sin,*
>   *and no deceit was found in his mouth."*
> *When they hurled their insults at him, he did not retaliate; when he suffered, he made no threats. Instead, he entrusted himself to him who judges justly. "He himself bore our sins" in his body on the cross, so that we might die to sins and live for righteousness; "by his wounds you have been healed." For "you were like sheep going astray," but now you have returned to the Shepherd and Overseer of your souls.*

══ Consider This ══

> To this you were called . . .

To what were we called? Back up a verse, and there it is: "But if you suffer for doing good and you endure it, this is commendable before God" (1 Peter 2:20).

We are called to suffer for doing good.

There it is. I have never said it so plainly to myself or anyone else.

We are called to suffer for doing good.

There is a technical term for this—*persecution.*

In the early centuries of the church, the primary hallmark of being a Christian was suffering for doing good. From the earliest days of the church, persecution was the rule, not the exception. In fact, in Jesus' most core teaching (aka the Sermon on the Mount), he put it this way:

"Blessed are those who are persecuted because of righteousness, for theirs is the kingdom of heaven. Blessed are you when people insult you, persecute you and falsely say all kinds of evil against you because of me. Rejoice and be glad, because great is your reward in heaven, for in the same way they persecuted the prophets who were before you." (Matthew 5:10–12)

Again, in John's gospel, Jesus says this:

"If the world hates you, keep in mind that it hated me first. If you belonged to the world, it would love you as its own. As it is, you do not belong to the world, but I have chosen you out of the world. That is why the world hates you. Remember what I told you: 'A servant is not greater than his master.' If they persecuted me, they will persecute you also. If they obeyed my teaching, they will obey yours also. They will treat you this way because of my name, for they do not know the one who sent me." (John 15:18–21)

This is the primary purpose for Peter's letter. He is not writing to tell the church to bow to the government. No, he's writing to encourage, teach, and train them how to prepare to suffer for doing good. That is the point of the whole letter. Here are Peter's pro tips for those under persecution:

- Do not retaliate.
- Do not threaten anyone.
- Entrust yourself to him who judges justly.

Suffering for doing good, according to the Bible, seems to be Christianity 101. So here's my honest question: Why am I not suffering for doing good? Maybe I have and am, so let me refine the question. Why am I not being persecuted? I am not aware of ever being persecuted for righteousness' sake in my whole life. Why is that? I don't experience being hated by the world. I don't recall anyone hurling insults at me because of my relationship to Jesus. Sure, I have suffered from what I would call spiritual warfare and demonic attacks and just bad things happening in my life, but I don't think that fairly qualifies as being persecuted for righteousness' sake, or suffering for doing good as Peter talks about.

Don't hear me wrong. I don't want to be persecuted. I am not asking for it. I suppose I am thankful I have not experienced it. I guess it makes me wonder why. I mean, if following Jesus means being persecuted and I am not being persecuted . . . well . . . logic presses me to ask the question: "Am I really following Jesus?" Maybe the better question might be, "How closely am I following Jesus?"

What if it is an issue of my location with respect to Jesus? He had three followers who were extra close to him—Peter, James, and John. It turns out they probably suffered the worst persecution. Then there were the other nine, all of whom reportedly died martyrs' deaths. Then there were the crowds. They followed more from a distance, didn't they? It would be hard to single someone out in a crowd. Perhaps that is the question I should be asking: "Am I following Jesus from up close as a disciple or from a distance in the nameless and faceless crowd?"

To this you were called . . .

The Prayer

Jesus, you are the Messiah, the Son of the living God. Thank you for the grace to honestly confront this issue of the lack of persecution in our lives and to ask these hard questions. We are not asking to be persecuted, Lord, but we do ask you to prepare us for such. Holy Spirit, should, or maybe I should say, when persecution comes to us, give us the grace to not retaliate or threaten but to entrust ourselves to him who judges justly. And prepare us for the blessedness of such a thing. Praying in Jesus' name. Amen.

The Questions

Have you ever been persecuted for righteousness' sake or for following Jesus or otherwise suffered for doing good? What's the story? Are you still following Jesus from the comforts of the anonymous crowd? Are you ready to step into more direct connection? Are you prepared for what that might mean by way of persecution?

1 Peter 3:1–6

27   The Problem with Equality

> *Wives, in the same way submit yourselves to your own husbands so that, if any of them do not believe the word, they may be won over without words by the behavior of their wives, when they see the purity and reverence of your lives. Your beauty should not come from outward adornment, such as elaborate hairstyles and the wearing of gold jewelry or fine clothes. Rather, it should be that of your inner self, the unfading beauty of a gentle and quiet spirit, which is of great worth in God's sight. For this is the way the holy women of the past who put their hope in God used to adorn themselves. They submitted themselves to their own husbands, like Sarah, who obeyed Abraham and called him her lord. You are her daughters if you do what is right and do not give way to fear.*

Consider This

> Wives, in the same way submit yourselves to your own husbands.

Most people struggle with this text and others like it because they read it through the lens of power differentials rather than within earshot of the empty tomb.

So why do we tend to read texts like these through the lens of power differentials? Because we tend to read the Bible more as American Christians than as Christian Americans. An American Christian is going to approach Scripture with the foundational assumption that all people are created equal. A Christian American is going to approach Scripture with the foundational assumption that all people are created in the image of God. I don't mean to eschew equality as somehow wrong or bad. It just may not be the primary value set in the kingdom of Jesus.

Equality is a social construct of comparison and, ultimately, of power, inevitably pitting human beings against one another. It is often the domain of the elite, whose interest tends to be either the maintenance of power or its redistribution. How does Jesus deal with power imbalances? In a word: *submission*. In another word: *cross-bearing*.

"So God created humankind in his image, in the image of God he created them; male and female he created them" (Genesis 1:27). Is equality a feature of the image of God? I would say that the pursuit of equality is actually a feature of the fallenness of human beings. Isn't this precisely where the original image bearers of God first went off the rails—when they grasped for equality with God in the Garden of Eden? Isn't there a tower somewhere out there on the ancient plains of Shinar, a tribute to equality, resting in the rubble of Babel, a tower with its top in the heavens (Genesis 11)? Is this not precisely the response and remedy of Jesus to the failed start of the original image bearers—Jesus, the Image of God himself, "who, being in very nature God, did not consider equality with God something to be used to his own advantage; rather, he made himself nothing" (Philippians 2:6–7)?

What if being created in the image of God has little to do with equality and everything to do with holy love, with profound submission to one another, with mutual deference, with regarding others as better than ourselves, with becoming last instead of first and least instead of greatest, even with laying down our lives for one another in love (see 1 John 3:16)?

I am not saying that equality among human beings is not a noble and grand aspiration for the unbelieving world to strive after, even in America. I'm just saying it is a painfully and pitifully low bar for the church Jesus is building and a foreign language to the kingdom of "on earth as it is in heaven." The agenda of the Word of God is not fighting power imbalances but subverting them through the counterintuitive strategy of cross-bearing.

The world is filled with despotic men and tyrannical women—it always has been. The church Jesus is building in the kingdom of "on earth as it is in heaven" is not of this world. We are not called to operate from the social justice engineers' playbook. They will forever be locked in a zero-sum, stalemated quest for power in the name of equality. The latest frameworks center around privilege and equity. Social engineers have become so prominent in our time because the institution posing as the church has been so anemically weak. We have even allowed the world to define the framework of the church in terms of equality, pitting the egalitarians against the complementarians. Friends of Jesus, we are witnessing in our time and on our watch the triumph of modern sociology and postmodern social theory over biblical theology and kingdom of God realism.

So what does any of this have to do with Peter's words about wives submitting to their husbands? And thank you for bearing with the long setup today. People tend, at best, to critique today's text and others like it and, at worst, reject them altogether. On the one hand, some dismiss them as the benign value set of an ancient Near Eastern culture with no present-day application. On the other hand, some brand them as the dangerous ideology of an oppressive patriarchy.

Friends, these are the revealed words of God. We do not sift them; they sift us. Peter is writing not from a worldly point of view but from a divine vantage point. We must labor to join his vantage point—which is in the company of Jesus, at the foot of the cross, in close proximity to the empty tomb. We must labor to leave behind the distorted vantage point of the mind of Adam, which is the decided pattern of this world, and read through the lens of the prismatic brilliance of the mind of Christ, which is given to us by the Holy Spirit. From this vantage point, I suggest to you that "wives, submit to your husbands" and "husbands, respect your wives" means something quite different from what our predisposed, power-saturated, world-shaped notions would lead us to think it means.

Jesus is after something so categorically beyond equality that it doesn't even live on the same spectrum. He is the one who said that if we want to be first, we must become the last, and if we want to become the greatest, we must become the servant of all. He is the one who, being in very nature God, made himself nothing and took on the nature of a slave. He is the one who said that if someone sues you for your shirt, give them your coat too. And if someone forces you to go with them one mile, go with them two. He is the one who looked straight in the face of the man who would pronounce his death sentence and said, "My kingdom is not of this world" (John 18:36).

(And just so you know I know, if you are a battered spouse in some kind of abusive relationship, don't walk—run. All bets are off.)

The Prayer

Jesus, you are the Messiah, the Son of the living God. We have learned a lot from this world and accepted so much of it uncritically. Teach us about your kingdom. We want our values to be sifted by the Word of God and sorted by the kingdom. Forgive us for getting that backward. Holy Spirit, fill us with the mind of Christ so that we might value what you value and think like you think. Praying in Jesus' name. Amen.

The Questions

Have you assumed that equality is the biblical standard? Where do you find this in your study of Scripture? How are you processing my claim today that there might be an even higher biblical standard than equality?

Week 4:
Discussion Questions

Hearing the Text: 1 Peter 2:11–3:6

Dear friends, I urge you, as foreigners and exiles, to abstain from sinful desires, which wage war against your soul. Live such good lives among the pagans that, though they accuse you of doing wrong, they may see your good deeds and glorify God on the day he visits us.

Submit yourselves for the Lord's sake to every human authority: whether to the emperor, as the supreme authority, or to governors, who are sent by him to punish those who do wrong and to commend those who do right. For it is God's will that by doing good you should silence the ignorant talk of foolish people. Live as free people, but do not use your freedom as a cover-up for evil; live as God's slaves. Show proper respect to everyone, love the family of believers, fear God, honor the emperor.

Slaves, in reverent fear of God submit yourselves to your masters, not only to those who are good and considerate, but also to those who are harsh. For it is commendable if someone bears up under the pain of unjust suffering because they are conscious of God. But how is it to your credit if you receive a beating for doing wrong and endure it? But if you suffer for doing good and you endure it, this is commendable before God. To this you were called, because Christ suffered for you, leaving you an example, that you should follow in his steps.

> "He committed no sin,
>> and no deceit was found in his mouth."

When they hurled their insults at him, he did not retaliate; when he suffered, he made no threats. Instead, he entrusted himself to him who judges justly. "He himself bore our sins" in his body on the cross, so that we might die to sins and live for righteousness; "by his wounds you have been healed." For "you were like sheep going astray," but now you have returned to the Shepherd and Overseer of your souls.

Wives, in the same way submit yourselves to your own husbands so that, if any of them do not believe the word, they may be won over without words by the behavior of their wives, when they see the purity and reverence of your lives. Your beauty should not come from outward adornment, such as elaborate hairstyles and the wearing of gold jewelry or fine clothes. Rather, it should be that of your inner self, the unfading beauty of a gentle and quiet spirit, which is of great worth in God's sight. For this is the way the holy women of the past who put their hope in God used to adorn themselves. They submitted themselves to their own husbands, like Sarah, who obeyed Abraham and called him her lord. You are her daughters if you do what is right and do not give way to fear.

Responding to the Text

- What did you hear?
- What did you see?
- What did you otherwise sense from the Lord?

Sharing Insights and Implications for Discipleship

Drawing from the Scripture text and daily readings, what did you find challenging, encouraging, provocative, comforting, invasive, inspiring, corrective, affirming, guiding, or warning?

Shaping Intentions for Prayer

Write your discipleship intention for the week ahead.

5
WEEK

---

1 Peter 3:7–18

29

1 Peter 3:7–12

Why Our Relationships Are the Mission

> *Husbands, in the same way be considerate as you live with your wives, and treat them with respect as the weaker partner and as heirs with you of the gracious gift of life, so that nothing will hinder your prayers.*
>
> *Finally, all of you, be like-minded, be sympathetic, love one another, be compassionate and humble. Do not repay evil with evil or insult with insult. On the contrary, repay evil with blessing, because to this you were called so that you may inherit a blessing. For,*
> > *"Whoever would love life*
> > > *and see good days*
> > *must keep their tongue from evil*
> > > *and their lips from deceitful speech.*
> > *They must turn from evil and do good;*
> > > *they must seek peace and pursue it.*
> > *For the eyes of the Lord are on the righteous*
> > > *and his ears are attentive to their prayer,*
> > *but the face of the Lord is against those who do evil."*

═══ Consider This ═══

One of the most impactful classes I took in seminary was a class on healing and prayer taught by the late great man of God Dr. Donald Demaray. We read a lot of books on the subject, but we spent most of our time actually praying together. Demaray would work his way around the altar, modeling how to pray for and minister to one another in healing prayer. As each prayer time began, he asked the one being prayed for this question: "Are the channels clear?" He was asking, in essence, "Are your relationships right?"

Peter is doing a similar thing, quite subtly but clearly, in his letter. Watch:

> Husbands, in the same way be considerate as you live with
> your wives, and treat them with respect . . . so that nothing
> will hinder your prayers.

He's saying, "Keep the channels clear"—which is another way of
saying, "Make your relationships right." Watch again:

> Whoever would love life
>   and see good days
> must keep their tongue from evil
>   and their lips from deceitful speech.
> They must turn from evil and do good;
>   they must seek peace and pursue it.
> For the eyes of the Lord are on the righteous
>   and his ears are attentive to their prayer.

Righteousness is fundamentally not about right behavior but about
right belonging to one another. It is about right relationships. This is why
slander, deceitful speech, and the bearing of false witness against others
are so devastatingly serious. A person can manage their behavior and
still not right their relationships. That is where self-righteousness comes
from. Self-righteousness is just the outworking of hard-heartedness.
People resist making their relationships right because they can't come
to grips with their own brokenness. Dr. Don was spot-on, wasn't he?
"Are the channels clear? Are your relationships right?"

Something tells me Peter took Jesus both literally and seriously
when he said things like this:

> "Therefore, if you are offering your gift at the altar and there
> remember that your brother or sister has something against
> you, leave your gift there in front of the altar. First go and be
> reconciled to them; then come and offer your gift." (Matthew
> 5:23–24)

And in case that wasn't clear enough, there was this:

"For if you forgive other people when they sin against you, your heavenly Father will also forgive you. But if you do not forgive others their sins, your Father will not forgive your sins." (Matthew 6:14–15)

Bottom line: keep the channels clear and make the relationships right—with Jesus, with yourself, within your marriage, with your children, with your friends and neighbors and colleagues, inside your organization, within the church, and even with enemies. Nothing hinders the mission of Jesus in the world more than broken relationships among his people and within his church. I say these words to the Farm Team at Seedbed all the time: our relationships are the mission—citing Jesus' prayer for us:

> "My prayer is not for them alone. I pray also for those who will believe in me through their message, that all of them may be one, Father, just as you are in me and I am in you. May they also be in us so that the world may believe that you have sent me." (John 17:20–21)

It's why Peter is always saying things like this in today's text:

> Finally, all of you, be like-minded, be sympathetic, love one another, be compassionate and humble.

You've heard it said that unforgiveness is like drinking poison and expecting it to kill the other person; yet the truth is that it poisons the well for everyone around. It's why Peter quoted Psalm 34:14: "Seek peace and pursue it."

The Prayer

Jesus, you are the Messiah, the Son of the living God. We hear you asking us, "Are the channels clear?"—even though you already know the answer. Would you search our hearts and show us these broken relationships and lead us to do our part to mend them? Making relationships right can feel so heavy, and yet it's such an easy burden for you to bear, so most of all, open our hearts to your softening Spirit. Remind us that so often the brokenness in our bodies is tied directly to the brokenness of our relationships, and such is the brokenness in your body. Holy Spirit, work healing in and among us. Praying in Jesus' name. Amen.

═══ The Questions ═══

So how are things in your relationships? Don't live in self-condemnation over your brokenness. In fact, renounce shame and condemnation. Can you begin to open yourself up to the willingness of Jesus to heal those relationships—in his way and in his time? Can you take even a small step in that direction today? He will lead you gently and wisely. So much depends on receiving healing. And it's just not worth it to hold on to the brokenness.

---

30 | 1 Peter 3:8–12

Does the Church Exist for Me, or Do I Exist for the Church?

> Finally, all of you, be like-minded, be sympathetic, love one another, be compassionate and humble. Do not repay evil with evil or insult with insult. On the contrary, repay evil with blessing, because to this you were called so that you may inherit a blessing. For,
>
> "Whoever would love life
>   and see good days
> must keep their tongue from evil
>   and their lips from deceitful speech.
> They must turn from evil and do good;
>   they must seek peace and pursue it.
> For the eyes of the Lord are on the righteous
>   and his ears are attentive to their prayer,
> but the face of the Lord is against those who do evil."

For the longest time, I have viewed letters like this one from Peter and others from Paul as miscellany in which they often appear to be responding to frequently asked questions concerning what God says about this social problem, that ethical issue, or this moral dilemma. And as a consequence, that's how I have typically read and interpreted them. What does the Bible say about same-sex relationships? What does the Bible say about money? What does the Bible say about marriage? Certainly, all these things and more are addressed over the course of the multiple correspondences that make up the New Testament. However, giving answers to these questions is not the main purpose and point of the New Testament.

We must keep the main point of the letter front and center—finding our place and playing our part in the church Jesus is building. These letters were written by apostles to churches for the sake of the spread of the kingdom of heaven across the earth.

Peter is not trying to give us a marriage seminar. He knows these churches are made up of families, but note his calculus is not "as goes the family, so goes the church." If that were the case, he would have dedicated the entire letter to family life. Peter knows the opposite is true: "as goes the church, so goes the family." So many times along the way I have heard people espouse a priority list something like this: (1) God; (2) family; (3) church. I suppose given the church as I have known it, this ordering makes sense. However, this ordering of priorities would make no sense to the New Testament writers. Here is how they would have ordered the list: (1) Jesus; (2) church; (3) kingdom of heaven on earth.

In the New Testament, the idea of somehow separating out family from church as a different category would have been absurd. Church would have been the covering and shelter for the family. The apostles are not dealing with a federation of loosely connected families; they are pouring everything they have into the body of Jesus Christ.

If you will notice, the central concern of the New Testament is not the individual believer or the nuclear family, but rather the supernatural community known as the church Jesus is building. And the central concern of the church Jesus is building is the relationships therein—Jews and Gentiles, slaves and masters, men and women, husbands and wives, parents and children. Every single relationship—and all of them together—matters more than we can possibly imagine within the body of Christ for the sake of the world.

> Finally, all of you, be like-minded, be sympathetic, love one another, be compassionate and humble.

And every single relationship and interaction with those outside of the body of Christ matters more than we can possibly imagine for the mission of the kingdom in the world.

> Do not repay evil with evil or insult with insult. On the contrary, repay evil with blessing, because to this you were called so that you may inherit a blessing.

Friends of Jesus, it's about relationships. The American Christian tends to believe and act as though the church exists for the sake of the flourishing of the individual and the family. In this model, the notion of the expansion of the kingdom of heaven on earth is an afterthought at best. The Christian American tends to believe and act as though the individual and the family exist for the sake of the flourishing of the church, whose mission is the expansion of the kingdom of heaven on earth.

If I'm honest, I have mostly thought of the church as existing for me. I'm finally waking up to the realization that I exist for the sake of the church—the one Jesus is building, that is.

The Prayer

Jesus, you are the Messiah, the Son of the living God. Thank you for the church you are building. We confess we have too often thought we could somehow do it better than you and have done it in our own way, claiming we've done it in your name. We seem so far from the New Testament church, as though we could somehow find it by our own resolve. We can't. And this is the point. Holy Spirit, bring us to humble honesty; deep, joy-filled repentance; and profound surrender to you and submission to one another. Praying in Jesus' name. Amen.

In what ways have you tended to believe that the church exists for the sake of individuals and families rather than the other way around? Reflect on those ways.

---

1 Peter 3:13–14

31

Why Evil Is Not the Real Problem

> *Who is going to harm you if you are eager to do good? But even if you should suffer for what is right, you are blessed. "Do not fear their threats; do not be frightened."*

Consider This

Peter has put down his clipboard and is going heart to heart with the team now. He has moved from coaching to pure encouragement. Hear today's text in that spirit and tone, and see if you agree.

I somehow think in the back of Peter's mind, this conversation with Jesus had to rise up in times like these when he was writing to Christians who were taking it on the chin for the kingdom. You will recognize the scene as the famous postresurrection seaside conversation.

> Jesus said, "Feed my sheep. Very truly I tell you, when you were younger you dressed yourself and went where you wanted; but when you are old you will stretch out your hands, and someone else will dress you and lead you where you do not want to go." Jesus said this to indicate the kind of death by which Peter would glorify God. Then he said to him, "Follow me!" (John 21:17–19)

Peter belonged to Jesus so completely that he had reached the level of Jesus' own invincibility. He knew it would not end well for him; he knew it would end gloriously! He knew his enemies couldn't kill a person who had already been raised from the dead. It made him untouchable by evil. Peter loved Jesus and trusted him so much he could stare death in the face and wink. This is a dangerous person to the kingdom of death and darkness. All the mafia of hell comes against a person like this, and they can't touch him. I wonder if these words of Jesus from that red-letter day at Caesarea Philippi continually reverberated through his heart and mind: "I tell you that you are Peter, and on this rock I will build my church, and the gates of Hades will not overcome it" (Matthew 16:18).

It takes a person like that to say things like this: "Who is going to harm you if you are eager to do good?"

And then Peter seems to catch himself, as if to answer his own question: "Actually, a lot of people are eager to harm you for doing good. In fact, the legions of hell are ever on the prowl for unwitting human minions to do their bidding." Then he adds this:

> But even if you should suffer for what is right, you are blessed. "Do not fear their threats; do not be frightened."

And let's not forget we are no longer dealing with amateur Pharisees and a junior varsity high priest. This is pure, unbridled, teeth-gnashing wickedness (aka Emperor Nero). "Do not fear their threats; do not be frightened," he dictates to Silas as he smiles. In my reading of Scripture and my life's experience, evil is not the problem for the church Jesus is building; fear is. We make a thousand mistakes when we give in to fear. Very good people do very bad things, not because they are evil, but because they are afraid. It's why Peter earlier exhorts us to live in reverent fear of God alone (which is a kind of fear that is not really afraid). On that point, let's give Apostle John the last word today: "There is no fear in love. But perfect love drives out fear, because fear has to do with punishment. The one who fears is not made perfect in love" (1 John 4:18).

The Prayer

Jesus, you are the Messiah, the Son of the living God. And on this rock you are building your church, and the gates of hell will not overcome it. Thank you for this mighty fortress—a bulwark never failing. We long to trust you more, Jesus. Jesus, how we trust you, how we've proved you over and over. Jesus, Jesus, precious Jesus, O for grace to trust you more![1] Lord, we don't want to play at this. We want to rise up into it. Perfect love, Jesus. You are perfect love. Holy Spirit, bring us perfect love. Praying in Jesus' name. Amen.

The Questions

What do you make of this point about evil not being the problem for us so much as fear? Does it ring true? Do you carry fear? Be honest with yourself. Are you ready for perfect love to drive out your fear?

---

32 | 1 Peter 3:15
The $64,000 Question of the Bible

> But in your hearts revere Christ as Lord.

Consider This

Now we get to Peter's secret. It's also Paul's secret. And it's Mary's secret, and the secret of Phoebe, and Hannah, and Silas, and John, and Allison, and Tangie, and Susanne, and Dan—and I could go on and on. But most importantly, it is *your* secret. It's right there in verse 15.

> But in your hearts revere Christ as Lord.

I don't like the term our translators chose here: *revere*. Of course, it's not wrong, but there are better options. In my mind, to revere something or someone is to look up to them or highly regard them. The Greek term is *hagiazo* (pronounced hag-ee-**ad**-zo). Peter dropped a form of this

---

1. See Louisa M. R. Stead, "'Tis So Sweet to Trust in Jesus" (1882). Public domain.

biblical bomb of a word earlier in 1:15–16: "But just as he who called you is holy, so be holy in all you do; for it is written: 'Be holy, because I am holy.'"

The word can be translated as "sanctify" or "set apart"—and here's my favorite: "consecrate."

This, of course, raises the $64,000 question—the ultimate question—of the whole Bible: *How?* How are we to be holy as God is holy? Today, Peter gives us the answer. I'll offer my own amplified version of the text: "But in your hearts—the innermost place in your innermost self—set apart, sanctify, consecrate, and revere Jesus Christ as Lord."

It means your heart is a sanctuary for Jesus, so give him full run of the place. Jesus is Lord, but we must actually grant him lordship at the very center of our lives. Jesus is King, but he must be exalted to the throne of our innermost selves.

That all sounds well and good, but how do we do that? Let's begin by saying how we don't do that. So many believe in what I call the replacement approach. Jesus wants to replace whatever it is I have centralized or given priority to in my life—be it disordered affections, dysfunctional desires, addictions, idols, or just garden-variety sin—but first I have to get rid of all these things. We try to change and maybe make a little progress, but it never really sticks. We settle for putting a bumper sticker on our hearts that reads, "I'm not perfect, just forgiven." And we go on to live self-indulgent and otherwise defeated lives while trying to mask our lethargic laziness with the activity of busyness. We have all done it, and some of us have broken free only to fall back into our tried-and-true strategies.

It's why we keep calling out to each other, "Wake up, sleeper, rise from the dead, and Christ will shine on you!"

If this is you, I have very good news today. Jesus doesn't work by replacement; he works by displacement. When Jesus Christ is set apart as Lord in our hearts and enthroned as King, he displaces our disordered affections, dysfunctional desires, idols, and garden-variety sin. His light displaces my darkness. His life displaces my death. His order displaces my chaos. His wholeness displaces my brokenness. His attentiveness displaces my distractedness. His joy displaces my despair. His peace displaces my anxiety. His fullness displaces my emptiness. His attachment displaces my addictions. We can stop giving all our energy and focus to the old broken self in our lives the minute we decide to really give him the run and reign of our heart. Give Jesus time and space, and he will fill us with all the fullness of God.

And here is where the word *revere* is not such a bad word. Once he is consecrated in our hearts, and our hearts to him—once he is set apart and enthroned as King—we can then revere him as Lord. We worship him, which is to say we humble ourselves in his sight and exalt him for all his worth.

And this is not a one-and-done kind of thing. This is the hidden habit of the consecrated heart. It is every day . . . every hour . . . every minute . . . until it has become the unconscious disposition of our souls, the fiery affection of our attention, indeed, the fulfilled desire of our longing heart. This is not practical, you say. And you are right. This is not practical. This is love. Let's give Isaac Watts the last word today:

> Were the whole realm of nature mine,
> that were an offering far too small.
> Love so amazing, so divine,
> demands my soul, my life, my all.[2]

The Prayer

Jesus, you are the Messiah, the Son of the living God. We confess that we have hacked at our sins for too long, like weeds that won't stop. It has not worked. The more we focus on our sin, the more we are focused on our sin. We are ready to turn the complete totality of our focus to you, Jesus. We want to consecrate you as Lord of our hearts. We think we may have done that before, but we want to do it again and again and again, until we have done it, and then do it again. You are so worth it, Jesus. Holy Spirit, open this way of displacement for us and give us the joy of seeing all that is old and broken in us displaced by you. Praying in Jesus' name. Amen.

---

2. Isaac Watts, "When I Survey the Wondrous Cross" (1707). Public domain.

Does this contrast between replacement and displacement help you? "Perfect love drives out fear." Isn't that another way of saying it? Jesus is perfect love, right?

33

1 Peter 3:15–17

Why the Best Defense Is a Good Offense

> *Always be prepared to give an answer to everyone who asks you to give the reason for the hope that you have. But do this with gentleness and respect, keeping a clear conscience, so that those who speak maliciously against your good behavior in Christ may be ashamed of their slander. For it is better, if it is God's will, to suffer for doing good than for doing evil.*

Consider This

Always be prepared to give an answer to everyone who asks you to give the reason for the hope that you have.

For decades now, I have seen this verse taught as the New Testament banner text for the work of apologetics. For those unfamiliar with the term, apologetics is the field of study wherein people develop reasoned arguments for or defenses of the Christian faith. One of its core principles is this: our heart cannot embrace what our mind rejects. Christian apologetics is a good thing, and this approach has helped many skeptics come to faith in Jesus Christ.

I just don't see that 1 Peter 3:15 has anything to do with the field of study that has come to be known as Christian apologetics. I'm willing to be wrong on this—and I don't really care to debate it—but Peter is dealing with people who are coming under withering enemy fire because of their allegiance to Jesus. They are suffering for doing good, being slandered and despised—even facing martyrdom. It just doesn't seem like Peter is telling them to make reasoned arguments defending the Christian faith to their detractors or somehow to help people get beyond their rational, intellectual objections to the existence of God. Or am I missing something?

> Always be prepared to give an answer to everyone who asks you to give the reason for the hope that you have.

The answer is Jesus. There is no other answer. The answer is not a doctrinal declaration but rather an evidentiary fact. The evidence is the witness of a person who has set apart Jesus as Lord in their heart. This person is a qualitatively different kind of person, and this difference is most purely proved in the midst of trials and hardships. It is most demonstrably proved when a person gladly suffers for doing good and returns good for evil.

Who does that? Jesus does. He is the answer to everyone who asks, and he is the reason for the hope we have. It's why the saying is true, "The best defense is a good offense." If you will notice, Jesus never played defense—always offense. Here is what's most confounding about Jesus: He wasn't playing to win; he was playing to lose. And that's how he won the victory of all victories. This is Peter's whole case. His entire case rests on one witness.

Peter is telling the Christian merchant in Bithynia who has just been publicly slandered and maligned because he follows Jesus to bless this person and pray for him and speak well of him in return. Then a neighbor asks this merchant why he didn't defend himself against them for this malicious attack and is further confounded by the Christian's stunning move to bless and not curse his enemy. Peter says to the maligned merchant, "This is your moment. When they ask, be ready to tell them your secret (à la 1 Peter 3:15). Oh, and one more thing—be respectful, even gentle about it."

Friends of Jesus, it's time to stop playing defense; it's time to play offense. And know this: we will lose a lot of games, but we will come out undefeated.

Now chew on this for the rest of the day:

> For the message of the cross is foolishness to those who are perishing, but to us who are being saved it is the power of God. . . . For the foolishness of God is wiser than human wisdom, and the weakness of God is stronger than human strength. (1 Corinthians 1:18, 25)

═══ The Prayer ═══

Jesus, you are the Messiah, the Son of the living God. You are the Rock of Ages. Thank you for the foolishness of the cross, for showing us that the way up is the way down, that the least is the greatest and the last is the first, and that in your kingdom, mountains are moved by faith, and love wins by losing. Holy Spirit, would you lead us to be prepared to give an answer to everyone who asks for the reason of our hope—not a pat answer or a religious answer, but an answer that radiates with the power of God? Teach us to play offense. Praying in Jesus' name. Amen.

═══ The Questions ═══

How do you deal with the confounding nature of Jesus, his gospel, and his kingdom? Are you prepared to share with others the reason for the hope you have?

34

1 Peter 3:18

The Truth about Doctrine

> *For Christ also suffered once for sins, the righteous for the unrighteous, to bring you to God. He was put to death in the body but made alive in the Spirit.*

Doctrine gets a bad rap. It gets portrayed as flat, fixed, and even fossilized truth. Nothing could be further from the truth. Doctrine is revelatory truth that has been crystallized, like a multifaceted diamond, into the brilliance of a refracted clarity. Doctrine never replaces Scripture, but it collects and collates these sacred texts into dynamic exhibits of revealed truth. Think of doctrine as a theological art gallery. Doctrine presents Scripture as a series of theological works of art.

This first letter of Peter alone is filled with all sorts of theological insights around the doctrine of atonement. First Peter 1:2 references the sprinkling of Jesus' blood. In 1 Peter 1:19, we are told we were not redeemed with perishable things, "but with the precious blood of Christ, a lamb without blemish or defect." Then in 1 Peter 2:24, we get this master stroke: "'He himself bore our sins' in his body on the cross, so that we might die to sins and live for righteousness; 'by his wounds you have been healed.'"

These texts give us the primary colors of the biblical doctrine of atonement. I have heard it described as "at-one-ment"—the bringing together of things that were divided into one again. "For 'you were like sheep going astray,' but now you have returned to the Shepherd and Overseer of your souls" (1 Peter 2:25).

Today's text speaks it as plain as day.

> For Christ also suffered once for sins, the righteous for the unrighteous, to bring you to God.

For all the great goodness of doctrine, there are at least two major pitfalls. On the one hand, we substitute doctrine for our experience, and on the other, we substitute our experience for our doctrine.

Part of the problem with doctrine is how over the years it has become like CliffsNotes on the Bible. It's like trying to reduce a movie to a series of still images. The Bible is like an epic movie series. Doctrines are like select scenes from the movie put into still images. The images only have meaning if you have seen the movie—and if you've seen the movie, they hold enormous significance.

Our doctrine, though, cannot be confused for our experience. Doctrine helps us understand and interpret our experience, but too often, it has been a substitute. We ask people to accept a set of doctrines when we need to be helping them encounter and experience Jesus Christ. Doctrine does not save people; only Jesus does that.

Then there is the peril of substituting our experience for our doctrine or, worse, defining our doctrine according to our experience. The deception of sin has shipwrecked many souls on the shoals of changing our doctrine to accommodate our broken human condition.

There is a supreme irony in the interplay of these two scenarios. Because we have been willing to allow an approach to doctrine that settles for mere acceptance instead of pressing on toward personal experience, we have perpetuated an approach to personal experience (whatever it may be) that elevates it to its own doctrine. In other words, the truth has been exchanged for "my truth" and "your truth."

I'll leave us in that perilous, ponderous place today.

The Prayer

Jesus, you are the Messiah, the Son of the living God. Holy Spirit, inspire in me a love for the glorious doctrine of our God. More than that, lead me into the experience of the truth. And save me from the futility of trying to define the truth according to my experience. Praying in Jesus' name. Amen.

The Questions

What is your experience of atonement?

Week 5:
Discussion Questions

Hearing the Text: 1 Peter 3:7–18

Husbands, in the same way be considerate as you live with your wives, and treat them with respect as the weaker partner and as heirs with you of the gracious gift of life, so that nothing will hinder your prayers.

Finally, all of you, be like-minded, be sympathetic, love one another, be compassionate and humble. Do not repay evil with evil or insult with insult. On the contrary, repay evil with blessing, because to this you were called so that you may inherit a blessing. For,

> "Whoever would love life
>   and see good days
> must keep their tongue from evil
>   and their lips from deceitful speech.
> They must turn from evil and do good;
>   they must seek peace and pursue it.
> For the eyes of the Lord are on the righteous
>   and his ears are attentive to their prayer,
> but the face of the Lord is against those who do evil."

Who is going to harm you if you are eager to do good? But even if you should suffer for what is right, you are blessed. "Do not fear their threats; do not be frightened." But in your hearts revere Christ as Lord. Always be prepared to give an answer to everyone who asks you to give the reason for the hope that you have. But do this with gentleness and respect, keeping a clear conscience, so that those who speak maliciously against your good behavior in Christ may be ashamed of their slander. For it is better, if it is God's will, to suffer for doing good than for doing evil. For Christ also suffered once for sins, the righteous for the unrighteous, to bring you to God. He was put to death in the body but made alive in the Spirit.

Responding to the Text

- What did you hear?
- What did you see?
- What did you otherwise sense from the Lord?

Sharing Insights and Implications for Discipleship

Drawing from the Scripture text and daily readings, what did you find challenging, encouraging, provocative, comforting, invasive, inspiring, corrective, affirming, guiding, or warning?

Shaping Intentions for Prayer

Write your discipleship intention for the week ahead.

6
WEEK

---

1 Peter 3:19–4:7

---

1 Peter 3:19

36

The Day Jesus Went to Hell

> *After being made alive, he went and made proclamation to the imprisoned spirits.*

═══ Consider This ═══

I grew up in a church that said the Apostles' Creed every Sunday. Even though I didn't fully understand it, I said it like I believed it, and it felt like it mattered. It feels even more so like it matters now. Let's affirm this ancient Creed of the Apostles now:

> I believe in God the Father Almighty,
> maker of heaven and earth;
> and in Jesus Christ, his only Son, our Lord:
> who was conceived by the Holy Spirit,
> born of the Virgin Mary,
> suffered under Pontius Pilate,
> was crucified, dead, and buried;
> he descended into hell.
> The third day he rose again from the dead;
> he ascended into heaven,
> and sits at the right hand of God the Father
>   Almighty;
> from there he shall come to judge the living and
>   the dead.
> I believe in the Holy Spirit,
> the holy catholic Church,
> the communion of saints,
> the forgiveness of sins,
> the resurrection of the body,
> and the life everlasting. Amen.

I'll never forget the first time as a kid when I was in another church where they, too, said the Apostles' Creed. It kind of made me feel like I belonged there too. Anyway, all was going well as I declared the ancient words from memory—until we came to this line: "was crucified, dead, and buried." At this point, as I was about to boldly declare, "The third day he rose again from the dead," the people around me headed in a completely different direction. They all said, "He descended into hell."

What the . . . heck. (Okay, you know what I wanted to say there.) My small Methodist Sunday school mind had been blown. Did they just say the word *hell*? In unison? In church? And did they just declare with gusto that Jesus had gone there? Where on earth did they get this? It had to be wrong.

"He descended into hell."

> After being made alive, he went and made proclamation to the imprisoned spirits.

This is the place the Old Testament calls Sheol. It is the place the New Testament sometimes refers to as Hades. It was understood as the place of residence of the souls and spirits of the departed dead. In the ancient mind, it was thought of, at least in a spiritual geographical sense, as under the earth. We can get into some pretty esoteric speculation quickly on this point, as again we are dealing with unknowable and unverifiable realities, so I will avoid that here.

On that first Holy Saturday, Jesus descended into hell to liberate the captive saints and to bring them into the communion of saints—the great cloud of witnesses. Abraham, Isaac, Jacob, Sarah, Rebekah, Rachel, Leah, the Hebrew midwives, Moses, Aaron, Hannah, Samuel, David, Bathsheba, and on and on we could go.

"He descended into hell."

In the next chapter, Peter adds this bit:

> But they will have to give account to him who is ready to judge the living and the dead. For this is the reason the gospel was preached even to those who are now dead, so that they might

be judged according to human standards in regard to the body, but live according to God in regard to the spirit. (1 Peter 4:5–6)

He descended into hell. The third day he rose again from the dead. He ascended into heaven. From there he shall come to judge the living and the dead.

I know we don't have all this difference between Sheol and Hades and heaven and hell fully sorted and figured out. And honestly, we won't on this side of eternity. Jesus does. He never lets go. And he never gives up.

The Prayer

Jesus, you are the Messiah, the Son of the living God. Thank you for descending into hell. Thank you for setting the captives free. Thank you for your justice. And thank you for your mercy, which is even greater than your justice. Praying in Jesus' name. Amen.

The Questions

Has the Apostles' Creed been a part of your life? Would you like it to be?

---

1 Peter 3:20–22

37

That Time Jesus Rode with Me in the Farm Truck

> . . . *to those who were disobedient long ago when God waited patiently in the days of Noah while the ark was being built. In it only a few people, eight in all, were saved through water, and this water symbolizes baptism that now saves you also—not the removal of dirt from the body but the pledge of a clear conscience toward God. It saves you by the resurrection of Jesus Christ, who has gone into*

> heaven and is at God's right hand—with angels, authorities and powers in submission to him.

══ Consider This ══

When I was a teenager trying to believe and behave, I developed an imaginative sense of the presence of Jesus. I worked on a farm in the summers and was assigned to the irrigation crew—a job I hated with a passion. At around fifteen or sixteen, I developed an extensive vocabulary and expansive command of cusswords. I would cuss the heat, the mosquitoes, the mud, my boots, the irrigation pipes, and even at times my cousin Lee. It became a habit.

As I drove the truck on the farm from field to field, I began to imagine Jesus sitting in the seat across from me. With this conscious awareness, I began to watch my mouth. My cussing began to dissipate. I didn't so much believe that God was going to get me for cussing as I developed a reverence for the presence of God and a desire to esteem and not willfully offend him. It became a strangely real phenomenon.

I love how one of the most celebrated biblical scholars and theologians of our time, N. T. Wright, put it as he spoke about the ascension of Jesus—reminding us that today there is a Jewish carpenter seated in the heavens. Looking back on the farm and those days of riding in the truck with Jesus, maybe I wasn't so far off—a Jewish carpenter was seated in the truck with me. It has me wondering something I less and less wonder and more and more believe—the heavens are not somewhere out there over the rainbow; they are all around us.

The heavens are not so much directionally up as they are through. Through can be up, but it is not limited to such. I believe the heavens are a created dimension of reality everywhere around us all the time. They are not invisible, but unseen. Note the difference. To say a person or thing is invisible is to say something about that person or thing—that they are constitutionally invisible. It is impossible to see them. To say a person or thing is unseen is to say something about us and our capacity (or lack thereof) to see and perceive.

The risen and ascended Lord Jesus Christ is not invisible. He is a real, physically embodied person who is unseen; however, he has been seen many times by many people, beginning with Stephen, the first martyr of the church (Acts 7:55–56).

In becoming a human being, God severely limited himself to being one person in one place at one time. In ascending into heaven, Jesus went from a single, secure place on earth to a place of transcendent omnipresence in the heavens and yet imminently local on the earth. In other words, Jesus ascended from here to there so he could be intimately and movementally present from there to everywhere.

Some of you are no doubt wondering, *How does he know this?* Let me be clear. I don't know this. I am not claiming these things have been somehow revealed to me. I claim no special or secret knowledge. This is my best biblically informed, theologically discerned thinking. These are my tentative working conclusions, and as always, I submit them humbly and make them subject to challenge, correction, and refinement.

So back to the farm and Jesus riding with me in the truck. I got to where I could almost see him. Something in me needed to have a sense of Jesus outside of me and yet near me before I could become more conscious of him present within me and at work through me. I think it is the same now. It's kind of like this: if you say a person is everywhere but not really somewhere, then it's really more like they are nowhere—which makes them more of an idea or a concept than a person.

We must get beyond our fuzzy notion of God as a nebulous spiritual force who is somehow omnipresent, omnipotent, and omniscient. This is the basis of endless myths, sacred cows, baseless human imaginings, sinister power grabs, and ridiculous projections of human brokenness onto God. Jesus is a real person in a real place.

In the meantime, there's this little jewel of a message tucked in at the end of 2 Corinthians 4: "So we fix our eyes not on what is seen, but on what is unseen, since what is seen is temporary, but what is unseen is eternal" (verse 18).

The Holy Spirit is stretching the fabric of my imagination; sanctifying this most supernatural, most human dimension of my personhood; and causing me to fix my eyes on what is unseen—in other words, to fix my eyes on Jesus.

The process also looks like this word from the Master himself: "Blessed are the pure in heart, for they will see God" (Matthew 5:8).

Jesus, you are the Messiah, the Son of the living God. Thank you for taking us into a realm of understanding even angels long to peer into. Save us from vain speculation. Gift us with an understanding that will foment love and cause your kingdom to flourish on earth as it is in heaven. We want to see Jesus. Holy Spirit, grant us a purity of heart, indeed, a holiness without which no one will see the Lord. Praying in Jesus' name. Amen.

===== **The Questions** =====

Have you ever seen Jesus?

---

1 Peter 3:20–22

38

Where Exactly Is Jesus?

> *. . . to those who were disobedient long ago when God waited patiently in the days of Noah while the ark was being built. In it only a few people, eight in all, were saved through water, and this water symbolizes baptism that now saves you also—not the removal of dirt from the body but the pledge of a clear conscience toward God. It saves you by the resurrection of Jesus Christ, who has gone into heaven and is at God's right hand—with angels, authorities and powers in submission to him.*

===== **Consider This** =====

Where is Jesus? And why does it matter?

Here is what Peter knew. In the midst of the disciples' last conversation with Jesus on earth, this happened. There were no goodbyes. Jesus told them the Holy Spirit was coming and explained some of what that would mean.

After he said this, he was taken up before their very eyes, and a cloud hid him from their sight. They were looking intently up into the sky as he was going, when suddenly two men dressed in white stood beside them. "Men of Galilee," they said, "why do you stand here looking into the sky? This same Jesus, who has been taken from you into heaven, will come back in the same way you have seen him go into heaven." (Acts 1:9–11)

So here's a question. Where is heaven? Let's go back to the beginning. I noticed something in recent years that I missed the first several hundred times I read the first verse of the first chapter of the Bible. "In the beginning God created the heavens and the earth" (Genesis 1:1).

I never noticed until recently how in the beginning God created the heavens. Creation is not just the earth, but also the heavens. Was the preexistent God not already in heaven before creation? Apparently not. This original creation of the heavens and the earth provided the habitat for God and God's image bearers to dwell together in relational union. My sense is the heavens were other than the earth and yet permeated the earth in an indivisible fashion that resulted in a garden of abundant flourishing.

I find it interesting how what we call "the fall" is nowhere named as such in the Bible, as far as I can tell. Biblically speaking, it seems like it should be called "the curse"; at least, curse describes the impact, and the primary effect was division and separation—the division between human beings and God, the division between human beings and other human beings (and within themselves), the division between human beings and the creation itself, and, finally, the division between the heavens and the earth. The flourishing epic of Eden ended with God in the heavens and his image bearers as exiles on earth.

The rest of the Bible reveals the circuitous, surprising story of God's plan to rescue his image bearers, reverse the curse, restore the union, and reunite the heavens and the earth. Here's an alliterative plotline for you: creation, curse, covenant, Christ, church, culmination.

So back to our question: Where is Jesus, and why does it matter?

"Men of Galilee," they said, "why do you stand here looking into the sky? This same Jesus, who has been taken from you into heaven, will come back in the same way you have seen him go into heaven."

Those first Christians didn't experience Jesus as a spiritual feeling. Jesus was not some intangible spiritual experience for them. He was a real physically embodied person—so knowing where he was mattered as much to them as knowing him personally. They understood the end of the age had broken in upon them. The end of the beginning had arrived. They now lived in the beginning of the end. The defeat of evil had dawned and enemies of God were being fashioned into his footstool.

We have essentially lost this whole concept in our time. I'll just say it. Jesus is real to us, but not like he was real to them. He is real to us primarily as a spiritual experience, a divine being with whom we have a sense of relationship in our hearts. And this is not bad; it's just not nearly enough. And it's not really the vision of the New Testament church Jesus is building and the kingdom he is bringing "on earth as it is in heaven."

Jesus Messiah sits enthroned in the heavens (a real place) at the right hand of the Father in a physical, albeit glorified, body made of human flesh, where he lives to intercede for all who follow him, reigning and ruling as the Lord of heaven and earth, as commander in chief of the angel armies, as the head of the church, the firstfruits of the resurrection, the firstborn from the dead—the sovereign King of all that is, was, and ever shall be, world without end. Amen.

So where is Jesus?

Jesus is just through the veil in the unseen realm known as the heavens. He is beyond our sight, yet closer than our breath. He is right here, right now.

The Prayer

Jesus, you are the Messiah, the Son of the living God. You are risen and exalted as the ascended God of heaven and earth. Open the eyes of our hearts and wake us up to the real reality. Holy Spirit, parse out all the implications of this mind-blowing reality for us. And let this revelation cause us to combust in worship. Praying in Jesus' name. Amen.

What thoughts are churning in your heart and mind in light of what Jesus is revealing to you just now? What connections is the Spirit making?

1 Peter 4:1–3

The Rest of Your Earthly Life

> *Therefore, since Christ suffered in his body, arm yourselves also with the same attitude, because whoever suffers in the body is done with sin. As a result, they do not live the rest of their earthly lives for evil human desires, but rather for the will of God. For you have spent enough time in the past doing what pagans choose to do—living in debauchery, lust, drunkenness, orgies, carousing and detestable idolatry.*

Consider This

It just leaps out at me today.

The rest of your earthly life.
The rest of my earthly life.
The rest of our earthly lives.

There is at least one thing that we who are reading this all have in common. We don't know how long that will be—the rest of our earthly lives.

The text lays out two options for living the rest of our earthly lives:

> As a result, they do not live the rest of their earthly lives for evil human desires, but rather for the will of God.

Will I live the rest of my earthly life "for evil human desires" or "for the will of God"?

Something in us wants to believe there is a third option, something in between. This is the great deception. This is why most people are not living the rest of their earthly lives for the will of God. Not many people would willingly identify themselves as living "for evil human desires." Many, however, are not confident they are living "for the will of God." In the end, however, there is only one reason a person would not be confident they are living "for the will of God." The reason is their evil human desires. Isn't any desire contrary to the will of God, in all fairness, considered an evil desire?

> For you have spent enough time in the past doing what pagans choose to do—living in debauchery, lust, drunkenness, orgies, carousing and detestable idolatry.

Part of our problem is we have become accustomed to measuring down. We live our lives according to what is acceptable instead of what is excellent. Isn't this Peter's challenge—stop lowering the bar to the lowest common denominator? That's what a pagan is, after all—someone who has adopted the standards of the world, someone who is content to blend in with the broken ways of the broken world.

"You have spent enough time," Peter says. That's it. Sin is a waste of time. In other words, Peter urges, don't waste your life. Let the past be in the past. Don't spend another minute in regret. Precious time remains. Don't waste it. Live for the will of God.

The rest of your earthly life.

The rest of my earthly life.

The rest of our earthly lives.

That begins now.

The Prayer

Jesus, you are the Messiah, the Son of the living God. Thank you for what remains of the rest of my earthly life. Awaken me to the possibilities it holds. I want to live the rest of my earthly life for the will of God. Holy Spirit, empower me to rise above the evil desires that plague me. Even more, shake me out of the slumber of my indifference. Praying in Jesus' name. Amen.

Take a moment to consider what would be possible if you were to live the rest of your earthly life for the will of God.

---

1 Peter 4:4–6

40 Judgment Is Real

> *They are surprised that you do not join them in their reckless, wild living, and they heap abuse on you. But they will have to give account to him who is ready to judge the living and the dead. For this is the reason the gospel was preached even to those who are now dead, so that they might be judged according to human standards in regard to the body, but live according to God in regard to the spirit.*

==== **Consider This** ====

It is fitting that Apostle 1-A—Peter—would keep drawing us deeper into the substance of the Creed of the Apostles. We have covered the death, the descent to the dead, the resurrection and ascension, and the return, and now we come to the judgment. According to tradition, each of the apostles wrote one article of the twelve articles of the creed.

> But they will have to give account to him who is ready to judge the living and the dead.

In the parlance of the version of the Apostles' Creed's of my youth, "Suffered under Pontius Pilate, was crucified, dead, and buried; he descended into hell. The third day he rose again from the dead; he ascended into heaven, and sitteth on the right hand of God the Father Almighty."

And then this theological lodestar: "From thence he shall come to judge the quick and the dead."

For the longest time, I understood "the quick" to mean "the fast"—as in, no one can outrun the judgment. Of course, no thanks to the King James Version, it means "the living." And yet it is true either way. No one outruns the judgment. Everyone must stand before the judgment one day. The judgment is real. Everyone must give an account.

Growing up, and for many years thereafter, I didn't understand this. I wanted to know why. I reasoned this way: If God is God, why couldn't God just dispense with the whole need for judgment? Why couldn't God forgive sin by fiat? Why did Jesus have to die to atone for sin? Why did sin have to create separation? Couldn't God just wave his hand and change all this?

Short answer: For God to be God, God has to be true to God's own nature. Scripture reveals to us God's nature as the fiery union of holiness and love. God's nature manifests itself in our experience as justice and mercy. God's justice is the manifestation of his holiness. God's mercy is the manifestation of his love.

Jesus Messiah, the Son of God, the image of God in human flesh, shows us the perfect union of holiness and love, of justice and mercy. Nowhere is this more poignantly concentrated than in his suffering on the cross. As Peter wrote earlier, "For Christ also suffered once for sins, the righteous for the unrighteous, to bring you to God" (3:18).

Holiness cannot abide sin, but love can cover it. The holiness of God cries out for justice; the love of God cries out for mercy. Hear how Paul captures this sacred calculus of redemption: "God made him who had no sin to be sin for us, so that in him we might become the righteousness of God" (2 Corinthians 5:21).

We cannot atone for our own sin. We cannot stand in the judgment. By virtue of being a member of the fallen human race, we stand under condemnation unless someone else can stand for us. The good news: there is one who stands for us—Jesus Messiah.

The Prayer

Jesus, you are the Messiah, the Son of the living God. Thank you for the cross. Thank you for taking our place and giving us pardon instead of penalty. Thank you for your holiness and your love, for your justice and your mercy. Thank you for the miracle of your life, death, resurrection, ascension, and return. Holy Spirit, increase my experience of the mercy of pardon. Praying in Jesus' name. Amen.

The Questions

Are you prepared for the judgment of God? Have you accepted and received the merciful pardon of Jesus Christ? If not, what are you waiting for?

41

1 Peter 4:7

The End of All Things

> *The end of all things is near.*

Consider This

There are a few ways we can go with today's text.

> The end of all things is near.

- **Way #1: Apocalyptic Anxiety.** The sky is falling. Everything is going to pot or to the dogs or to Hades or however you tend to say such things. It is not hard to watch the news and then read select texts, like 1 Peter 4:7, and get all stirred up that the end is upon us and then leverage all this into what I call apocalyptic anxiety.

  This is where modern military weaponry gets interpreted through the lens of the biblical imagery of locusts and beasts and the temperature gets turned up in church (especially on TV). People will respond to this, once or twice, but after that, not so much. It is fairly easy to interpret the Bible according to the times in which we live. It can generate spiritual momentum and religious urgency . . . at least for a while.

- **Way #2: Apathetic Indifference.** Apocalyptic anxiety usually leads to apathetic indifference. Here's how it works. The end does not come. Things often get worse. The end still does not come. People get tired. Things don't get much better, but the calamity relents. The unsustainable fervor that launched 24-7 houses of prayer wanes. What began as hundreds on fire becomes a small circle of "the faithful" who never say die until they actually do. And God bless them, because though their fire burned down to embers, they kept the fire burning. Meanwhile, most everyone around them slowly drifted off to sleep. They didn't mean to. Many ran the first mile. Some ran the second, but most tuckered out and went back to their regularly scheduled lives, doing their best to stay faithful in the chaos of life.

  Apathetic indifference does not come all at once, and it happens to the best of us. It's not our fault. We responded to the fiery leadership of well-meaning, anxious leaders who are also most often very good people. I know this because I have been on both sides of this equation (as follower and leader). Apathetic indifference does not happen by decision but by declension. The lights dim slowly, giving our eyes ample time to adjust. Our faith quietly drifts back into a collection of beliefs.

  Apathy usually doesn't come from laziness but from unsustainable activity that has led to discouragement and disappointment. Faith doesn't go away so much as it suffers erosion. Faith doesn't die; it just becomes sleepy and domesticated.

- **Way #3: Eschatological Hope.** Rather than interpreting the Word of God in light of the times, we must learn to interpret the times in light of the Word of God. There is no question the first Christians and their apostolic leaders believed the end of all things was upon them. Why? It was not because of all of the craziness going on around them—nothing new about that. They believed the end of all things was near because something so unbelievably new had happened that it could only have signaled the dawning of a new age—the resurrection and ascension of Jesus Messiah and the coming of the Holy Spirit on the earth. These were the flashing—no, blazing—signs revealing this reality.

Then and now, biblical Christians understand time in two primary epochs: (1) the present evil age, and (2) the glorious age to come. Peter did not write these words—"The end of all things is near"—out of some kind of apocalyptic anxiety that the world was going to hell in a handbasket. No, he wrote them out of the deepest well of hope this side of heaven because it actually *was* anchored in heaven—eschatological hope. *Eschatology* is a twenty-five-dollar word that means "the doctrine of last things." The resurrection of the dead is the definitive sign of both the end of the beginning (the curse of sin and death) and the beginning of the end—"Where, O death, is your victory?" and "Where, O death, is your sting?" (1 Corinthians 15:55).

> The end of all things is near.

Why? One reason: Jesus Messiah is risen from the dead, firstborn from among the dead, the firstfruits of the resurrection. The glorious age to come has dawned. The future has broken in on the present evil age.

Translation: Hope is not in the future; it is from the future. The future has now dawned in the present.

> The end of all things is near.

I want you to draw two overlapping circles (like a two-circle Venn diagram). Label the circle on the left the "present evil age." Label the circle on the right the "glorious age to come." Now label the overlapping part of the two circles "the end of all things is near" (aka right now).

We are living in the overlap. The glorious age to come, the age of the Spirit, the age of the church, has broken in on the present evil age. We might also call it the "epic age of the mercy of God" and the "era of the salvation of Jesus Messiah." In other words, we are now living at the end of the age. We know this not because of cataclysm, calamity, or tragedies, which happen in every age. We know it because the definitive event has happened, signaling the end of the beginning and the beginning of the end—the resurrection and ascension of Jesus of Nazareth, the Messiah.

The God of heaven and earth plays the long game of eschatological hope. Think of how much time elapsed in circle #1, the present evil age—thousands of years. Now think of how much time will elapse in circle #2. It will not ultimately even be measured in time, for at the end of all things, time will give way to immeasurable eternity.

So no matter how long the period of time represented by the overlap of the ages is, in the scheme of things it will be short. It's why two thousand years later, Peter's word is as certain now as it was then:

> The end of all things is near.

According to the calendar of the triune God, it has only been a couple of days.

═══ The Prayer ═══

Jesus, you are the Messiah, the Son of the living God. You are risen, ascended, exalted, and reigning. And your mercy is over all your works. The end of all things is near. Holy Spirit, draw near and save us from the fear-filled anxiety of apocalypticism. Lead us to drink deeply from the heavenly well of eschatological hope. Awaken us from our apathy, from our sluggish slumber, and into this radiant hope that awakens the world. Praying in Jesus' name. Amen.

═══ The Questions ═══

How about you? Where do you find yourself right now? Apocalyptic anxiety? Apathetic indifference? Eschatological hope? Is there a fourth option? Are you seeing the differences? Have you struggled with the long period of waiting for the Lord's return? Or have you become more indifferent and even apathetic? Or is eschatological hope rising up in you?

Week 6:
Discussion Questions

Hearing the Text: 1 Peter 3:19–4:7

After being made alive, he went and made proclamation to the imprisoned spirits—to those who were disobedient long ago when God waited patiently in the days of Noah while the ark was being built. In it only a few people, eight in all, were saved through water, and this water symbolizes baptism that now saves you also—not the removal of dirt from the body but the pledge of a clear conscience toward God. It saves you by the resurrection of Jesus Christ, who has gone into heaven and is at God's right hand—with angels, authorities and powers in submission to him.

Therefore, since Christ suffered in his body, arm yourselves also with the same attitude, because whoever suffers in the body is done with sin. As a result, they do not live the rest of their earthly lives for evil human desires, but rather for the will of God. For you have spent enough time in the past doing what pagans choose to do—living in debauchery, lust, drunkenness, orgies, carousing and detestable idolatry. They are surprised that you do not join them in their reckless, wild living, and they heap abuse on you. But they will have to give account to him who is ready to judge the living and the dead. For this is the reason the gospel was preached even to those who are now dead, so that they might be judged according to human standards in regard to the body, but live according to God in regard to the spirit.

The end of all things is near. Therefore be alert and of sober mind so that you may pray.

Responding to the Text

- What did you hear?
- What did you see?
- What did you otherwise sense from the Lord?

Sharing Insights and Implications for Discipleship

Drawing from the Scripture text and daily readings, what did you find challenging, encouraging, provocative, comforting, invasive, inspiring, corrective, affirming, guiding, or warning?

Shaping Intentions for Prayer

Write your discipleship intention for the week ahead.

7
WEEK

---

1 Peter 4:7–16

1 Peter 4:7

43

What Is Prayer?

The end of all things is near. Therefore, be alert and of sober mind so that you may pray.

=== **Consider This** ===

There is a beautiful story from years ago about an interview Dan Rather did with Mother Teresa. He was asking her about prayer: "When you pray, what do you say to God?" She replied, "I don't say anything. I listen." He then prodded further: "What is it that God says to you when you pray?" She responded, "He also doesn't talk. He simply listens." Then she wryly added, "And if you don't understand that, I can't explain it."[1]

We all have some notion of prayer and some practice of it. It is time to take the notion deeper and the practice to the next level. What is prayer? The term Peter deploys here is *proseuchē* (pronounced pros-yoo-**khay**). We see it thirty-seven times throughout the New Testament. *Proseuchē*, or prayer, is a convergence of place, disposition, and activity, conveying more than a mere functional practice but getting at an overall orientation and way of being with God, in Christ, for the world.

Prayer is the way our relationship with Jesus shifts from casual acquaintance to deep knowing and from unfocused stuckness to movemental action in the world. It is an ongoing, cyclical movement beginning with awareness, rising into attention, becoming attunement, and settling into a deeply secure attachment to Jesus and others. There is a biblical term for the whole process—*abiding*.

See why wakefulness, watchfulness, and sobriety figure so prominently in all of this? This is the deepest essence of the church Jesus is building—a chosen people, a royal priesthood, a holy nation, God's special possession.

---

1. See Dan Rather, *The Other Journal: Prayer* (Eugene, OR: Cascade, 2013), ix.

> The end of all things is near; therefore, be of sound judgment and sober spirit for the purpose of prayer.

This is how Jesus saves the world. He calls us to join him. There's an urgency without anxiety, a power without striving.

══ The Prayer ══

Jesus, you are the Messiah, the Son of the living God. We see in you the life that is possible for us—not because we can somehow bring it about, but because you would willingly and willfully live in and through us. Lead us into this way of awareness, attention, attunement, and attachment that becomes the fiery, illumined life of abiding prayer. Holy Spirit, you are ever whispering this invitation to my spirit. Awaken me to hear it. Bring me into the sober intoxication of this kind of life I was made for. Praying in Jesus' name. Amen.

══ The Questions ══

Do you sense the Lord calling and leading you to a deeper and richer way of prayer? Don't let it be a burden on you. Consider it an invitation. Don't launch into a lot of activity. Just tell him you receive the invitation and ask for the next step of guidance.

---

1 Peter 4:8

44 Toward a Doctrine of Love

> *Above all, love each other deeply, because love covers over a multitude of sins.*

══ Consider This ══

We have a doctrine of the Trinity. We have a doctrine of salvation. We have a doctrine of the Holy Spirit. There are doctrines around eschatology, creation, sin, justification, sanctification, Scripture—and on and on we could go. But I have never seen a doctrine of love.

Is it just assumed? If so, how could we make such an assumption? Love is the central and defining reality—the sine qua non—of the Christian faith. What is the greatest commandment, after all? It is the one thing without which everything else (assuming we have everything else) constitutes utter mission failure.

> Above all, love each other deeply, because love covers over a multitude of sins.

We all have some notion of what we think it means to *love each other deeply*. Surely we can be honest, though, and admit that our definition of love is far more shaped by our culture than by hard-core theological truth. It's interesting how the dictionary has four or five different definitions for the same word—*love*—most of which center around human feelings. Meanwhile, the Bible has four or five completely different words for love, all of which we collapse into the one already confused English word we call *love*.

> Above all, love each other deeply, because love covers over a multitude of sins.

Above all, friends. *Above all*. Wouldn't we want to make this the focus of our extreme interest and the passionate focus of the "rest of our earthly lives"?

> Love each other deeply.

Paul contributes significantly to our doctrine of love by telling us what love is and what it is not (1 Corinthians 13):

> Love is patient.
> Love is kind.
> It does not envy.
> It does not boast.

It is not proud.
It does not dishonor others.
It is not self-seeking.
It is not easily angered.
It keeps no record of wrongs.

Even more so, a doctrine of love must tell us why. Our text today gives us one of the whys.

> . . . because love covers over a multitude of sins.

Here's another why from John: "Dear friends, let us love one another, for love comes from God. Everyone who loves has been born of God and knows God. Whoever does not love does not know God, because God is love" (1 John 4:7–8).

The kind of love Peter speaks about is an otherworldly, supernatural, transcendent kind of reality. In fact, this kind of love cannot be somehow separated from God, for it is God's very nature. It cannot be reduced to an ethical code; though it can be commanded, it cannot be conscripted. The only possible way for a human being to love as God loves is actually to share in the very nature of God. This brings us to the most important thing Peter ever said. It comes from his second letter.

> His divine power has given us everything we need for a godly life through our knowledge of him who called us by his own glory and goodness. Through these he has given us his very great and precious promises, so that through them you may participate in the divine nature, having escaped the corruption in the world caused by evil desires. (2 Peter 1:3–4)

Did you spot the miracle?

> . . . you may participate in the divine nature . . .

I cannot possibly convey the earthshaking consequence of these seven words. Because it is too easy to roll right past the English words, let's look at the original language through which they came into revelation: *genēsthe theias koinōnoi physeōs*.

Out of reverence, let's say it like the writer may have heard it in his mind as he wrote: **ge**-ney-sthe **thay**-os koy-no-**noy foo**-se-os.

- *genēsthe*—to become, to be born into or come into being, or to change condition, state, or place.
- *theias*—God's divine nature or essence.
- *koinōnoi*—a participant or partaker who mutually belongs and shares fellowship.
- *physeōs*—the inner nature or the underlying constitution or makeup of someone or something.

This is the miracle. As we abide together in Jesus Messiah, through the fellowship of the Holy Spirit, we partake of and participate in the very nature and essence of God—which is love. This is how "Above all, love each other deeply, because love covers over a multitude of sins" works—on earth as it is in heaven. When the miracle happens, the miracles happen. This is the whole point and purpose of the second half of the gospel.[2]

Genēsthe theias koinōnoi physeōs (**ge**-ney-sthe **thay**-os koy-no-**noy foo**-se-os). Why do I persist in using these unintelligible words? Because this is how we must approach this emerging doctrine of love—like we know nothing and must become beginners again and again and again. There is so much unlearning and relearning as so much human brokenness obscures this truth.

This is like a new language. Love is the mother tongue of heaven, meant to be spoken fluently on earth. I submit that if discipleship to Jesus is not about learning and becoming this distinctive kind of love, then it is about nothing at all.

---

2. See page 17. Also, go back to chapter 5, where the idea of "the second half of the gospel" is further explained.

Jesus, you are the Messiah, the Son of the living God. You are divine love simultaneously deified and personified, and in this way you show us the way. When you invite us to abide in you, you are inviting us to become partakers— participants in your very nature. Holy Spirit, koinonia of heaven, increase our yearning for this truth to become the most real thing in our lives. Lead us into this way, into this truth, into this life. Praying in Jesus' name. Amen.

The Questions

Is your heart waking up to a deeper longing to be filled to the measure of all the fullness of God, which is his love becoming power in and through us? If so, fan that flame. If not, keep kindling. As a symbolic exercise, learn and practice saying these four words from the Greek language: *genēsthe theias koinōnoi physeōs* (**ge**-ney-sthe **thay**-os koy-no-**noy** **foo**-se-os).

45

1 Peter 4:8

How Love Covers Sin

> *Above all, love each other deeply, because love covers over a multitude of sins.*

Consider This

When I was ten years old, I stole a twenty-dollar bill from my mother's purse. I took it to the backyard, threw it on the ground, walked about ten yards away, and then walked back over and picked it up again. After this, I rushed into the house and gleefully reported the good news to my mother. "Look what I found!" My mother, I should say, was no June Cleaver. Although uncertified, she is an accountant's accountant. It took her approximately thirty seconds to get to her purse and expose the fraud. After pleading guilty, I was arrested and put in a holding cell (my room) to contemplate my crimes while awaiting sentencing (when Dad got home). I could feel the fires of hell kindling around me.

Did I mention the planned fishing trip on the docket for that afternoon? I was crushed. Even the minimum sentencing guidelines would crush that plan, if not add weeks of grounding and likely a good old-fashioned spanking. Yep, kids, that's how it used to be in the old days.

Dad came in early for lunch that day. Mom and Dad entered my cell for the presentencing conference. Stern discussions ensued around lying, stealing, cheating, dishonoring parents, and the rest of the Ten Commandments. I had no case, no mitigating circumstances, no excuse—only tears. Then they handed down the sentence: pardon. The penalty? Time served. My contrition was met with their compassion. My flagrant foul was met with their forgiveness. My tearful transgression was met with merciful love. Their love covered my sins. And then Dad said, "Let's go fishing."

> Above all, love each other deeply, because love covers over a multitude of sins.

I wonder if when he wrote these words, Peter was thinking about that day on the shore of the Sea of Galilee when Jesus forgave his disloyal denials, set him free from his failures, and embraced him with the undeserved favor of grace.

Love covers sin. Your sin, my sin, our sin, a multitude of sins, indeed the sin of the whole world. Love covers sin. We all need constant reminding, and this comes from God as we love each other deeply, in the face of our falls and failures.

> Above all, love each other deeply, because love covers over a multitude of sins.

Do you know this kind of love that surpasses knowledge? Some reading this are sitting in their cell at this very moment, literally and figuratively, wondering if there is more than they have known. Pardon is only the tip of the iceberg. There is peace, purpose, power, provision—all of it carried in the overwhelming, never-ending, unfathomable love of God.

The Prayer

Jesus, you are the Messiah, the Son of the living God. Your love is better than life. I want to know this love fully, even as you fully know me. I want to know it beyond knowledge or a concept. I want to grasp how high and how wide and how deep and how long is your love, which is your bearing of goodness and grace toward us. I want this love to become my love for others. Holy Spirit, lead me to become this kind of carrier of the love of God. Praying in Jesus' name. Amen.

The Questions

Where are you on a scale of 1 to 10 in your own knowing experience of the love of God in Jesus Christ (with 10 being highest)? Do you believe it is possible for you to love with the love of God?

46

1 Peter 4:9–11

Loving beyond Our Exhausted Strength and into the Capacities of God

Offer hospitality to one another without grumbling. Each of you should use whatever gift you have received to serve others, as faithful stewards of God's grace in its various forms. If anyone speaks, they should do so as one who speaks the very words of God. If anyone serves, they should do so with the strength God provides, so that in all things God may be praised through Jesus Christ. To him be the glory and the power for ever and ever. Amen.

Consider This

Each of you should use whatever gift you have received to serve others, as faithful stewards of God's grace in its various forms.

What gift have you received?

You have a special Holy Spirit–given capacity to offer to the church Jesus is building. It is not a "spiritual gift," as they are commonly called. The Greek word is *charisma*, and it means grace-gifts. These grace-gifts are specific capacities and particular expressions of the supernatural love (*agape*) of God, given by the Holy Spirit to the followers of Jesus for the blessing and benefit of one another. They are ways and means by which we participate in and express the nature, presence, and power of God within and beyond the body of Christ. They are not necessarily functional talents or things you are, naturally or by practice, good at.

Over the years, the church we are building has functionalized and pragmatized the notion of the gifts of the Spirit. Many of you have taken spiritual gifts inventories that score your gifts. Local churches often use these kinds of tools to match and involve people in particular program-related ministries and missions of the church. The use of these tools is not wrong. I just don't think they works particularly well.

The gifts of the Spirit are not functional abilities. Rather, they are divine capacities. A gift of the Holy Spirit is a *transcendent* capacity to work in a particular way. It is to operate in the very same way Jesus operated, which is why I think the very best research concerning the grace-gifts of the Spirit comes from studying Jesus himself.

We can find many such dimensions of these gifts, ranging from showing mercy and serving others to speaking prophecy and performing miracles. Peter identifies a range from prophetic speech to waiting tables in today's text. So what is Peter doing here? We must remember verse 8 before considering verse 9: "Above all, love one another deeply, because love covers over a multitude of sins."

> Offer hospitality to one another without grumbling.

Hospitality here likely refers to taking in Christians they didn't know (i.e., strangers likely fleeing persecution) for meals and overnight lodging from other towns with no notice. Biblical hospitality, contrary to hospitality's current Martha Stewartization, is not about special guests you invite into your home to entertain. It's about the people you didn't invite who you may not know who show up at your door. This is the stuff that makes us grumble, right?

> . . . they should do so with the strength God provides.

Peter is calling us out as a people whose efforts to follow Jesus in our own strength and with our own resources have led us to depletion. He reminds us that we are part of a supernatural community that operates from a wealth of divine capacities—Spirit-given grace-gifts. In other words, he is saying to us something like, "Stop trying to do all this in your own strength. No wonder you are grumbling. Your love is of human origin. You must level up (or down, as the case may be) to the love that is of divine origin."

> . . . so that in all things God may be praised through Jesus Christ. To him be the glory and the power for ever and ever. Amen.

The Prayer

Jesus, you are the Messiah, the Son of the living God. You are the giver, and you are the gift. In fact, you show us what it looks like when all of the capacity of Almighty God shows up in a human being. Jesus, you are the gift, and you show us the gifts and how they operate. Holy Spirit, would you train us in the ways you are gifting us? We want to be in step with the power of your divine capacities and always in the deep love of God. Praying in Jesus' name. Amen.

The Questions

How have you related to the Holy Spirit–given gifts of grace? How do you think you have misunderstood them in the past? Do you have a sense of the gift you have received? What has that been like for you?

47

1 Peter 4:12–16

Do We Belong to Jesus? Or Do We Really Belong to the World in Jesus' Name?

Dear friends, do not be surprised at the fiery ordeal that has come on you to test you, as though something strange were happening to you. But rejoice inasmuch as you participate in the sufferings of Christ, so that you may be overjoyed when his glory is revealed. If you are insulted because of the name of Christ, you are blessed, for the Spirit of glory and of God rests on you. If you suffer, it should not be as a murderer or thief or any other kind of criminal, or even as a meddler. However, if you suffer as a Christian, do not be ashamed, but praise God that you bear that name.

Consider This

Under Nero, Christians were under severe persecution, even to the point of being crucified, torn by dogs, and burned. They were mocked as haters of humankind, ridiculed, and even tortured throughout the Roman Empire simply for identifying as Christians. Peter says to them something we need to hear today.

> Do not be surprised at the fiery ordeal that has come on you to test you, as though something strange were happening to you.

He effectively tells them persecution is a sign they are "doing it right." Persecution is the rule, not the exception. Stop being surprised by haters. It's interesting how these early Christians were called haters by the world around them. The irony is they were actually people of deep and profound love. The world hated them for this because their lives, simply by being light, stood in stark contrast to the world and its darkness.

I suspect Peter was remembering this lesson from Jesus: "If the world hates you, keep in mind that it hated me first. If you belonged to the world, it would love you as its own. As it is, you do not belong to the world, but I have chosen you out of the world. That is why the world hates you" (John 15:18–19).

On the regular, I hear from friends around the world who are actively experiencing this reality. It gives me no pleasure to warn those of us in the United States that this will increasingly become the case for us—at least in the church Jesus is building among us. We are in the early stages of a great pruning of the church in America. Having come through the long winter of Christendom, a period wherein the church effectively pushed its will on the state (and vice versa), we find ourselves waking up in the ruins.

Though this period gave many gifts to the world, its lasting legacy is lifeless institutions that are Christian in name only—nominally Christian (and often quite well-endowed) organizations that carry forms and vestiges of religion while denying its reality and power. Sadly, so many local churches fall into this category—advancing forms of godliness while denying the power of God. And so many of us, clergy and laity alike, are caught in the machinations of their motions.

Do we belong to Jesus? Or do we really belong to the world in Jesus' name? This is the pruning I refer to. I see two primary issues: meddling and false teaching. Broadly speaking, *meddling* attempts to conform the world to the values of the church, while *false teaching* attempts to conform the church to the values of the world. Meddling trends toward conservatism; false teaching trends toward progressivism.

Both approaches create rot from the inside out. Finally, and at risk of offending virtually everyone and their mother, we see the massive fault lines of these strategies exposed prominently across the church in the present-day highly confusing matters of sexuality and gender and to a lesser degree in matters of race and diversity. Both strategies (i.e., conservatism and progressivism) seem reasonable, plausible, and even godly to their adherents, but neither is a viable strategy for the church Jesus is building. The church must have *biblical theology*, period.

Jesus is not building his church on the fault lines of the ideological framework of conservatism or progressivism. This is where we are so stuck—drifting toward legalism on one side and license on the other. Ideologies inexorably lead to idolatries. This is why our churches have fallen deaf, blind, and mute—just like the idols they salute. And idolatry inevitably leads to injustice. What we are experiencing now across the church in America is not persecution but infighting. The persecution is coming.

This is why Peter will soon remind us that judgment must begin with the house of God. Jesus builds his church on one thing alone—the rock of Peter's wholehearted confession: "You are the Messiah, the Son of the living God." And as Peter told us earlier, Jesus will be either the cornerstone or the stumbling block. There is no in-between. As Hudson Taylor famously said, "Christ is either Lord of all, or is not Lord at all."

This is why the world hates Christians.

> However, if you suffer as a Christian, do not be ashamed, but praise God that you bear that name.

The Prayer

Jesus, you are the Messiah, the Son of the living God. We don't too much sense that the world hates us. It leaves us wondering if maybe we belong to the world and don't even know it. If we are honest, we're not sure we want to be hated by the world. We are open though. We want to belong to you so completely that we are actually sharing in the fellowship of your suffering, becoming like you in your death. This is a mystery, Jesus. Holy Spirit, bring us into the mystery, for we know this is life in the glory of God. Praying in Jesus' name. Amen.

The Questions

Have you ever been referred to as a "hater" for standing on biblical values and convictions? How do you deal with this? What might a humble approach look like?

1 Peter 4:15–16

48

The Problem with Meddlers

> *If you suffer, it should not be as a murderer or thief or any other kind of criminal, or even as a meddler. However, if you suffer as a Christian, do not be ashamed, but praise God that you bear that name.*

=== **Consider This** ===

Many have heard or used the phrase referencing a preacher whose message forays too deeply into their personal issues: "That preacher just went from preaching to meddling." It's a colloquial way of saying the preacher has gone too far. In reality, it more likely means the hearer has come under the conviction of the Holy Spirit.

The Greek word *allotriepiskopos* (al-loh-tree-eh-**pee**-sko-pos—don't even try) is used only once in the Bible. It means interfering or intruding into matters beyond one's own business. In this instance, it looks to be a reference to Christians trying to enforce their standards or values on unbelieving Gentiles. Peter seems to be saying something like this: "When you try to enforce the way of Jesus on people who don't follow Jesus and those people push back—that doesn't count as persecution. You had it coming."

Why do we Christians tend to carry an expectation that people who don't follow Jesus should act like Jesus? And why are we surprised when they don't? How could they possibly be like Jesus when they don't even know him? This is one of the vestiges of Christendom. America was never a Christian nation, because a nation can't be Christian. Only people can be Christian.

America was founded on Christian, deistic, and other congruent philosophical ideals. However, we have long since left that building. In other words, America may look and feel more like first-century Rome than 1776 America. We were founded on a social contract, a bit of an uneasy alliance among people who believed heartily in the risen Jesus

Christ, those who loosely subscribed to the concept of a distant God, and those who believed in Enlightenment rationalism alone. This was the center that more or less held for two hundred years. Unfortunately, the social contract has imploded. This center no longer holds.

For most of American history, the church has enjoyed a favored place in this country. In fact, the church has in many ways played a role as the benevolent host of the country. Our pledges, our anthems, and even our money reference "God." As the social contract has disintegrated and the center has collapsed, the American culture has diffused into an ever-evolving plethora of subcultures. Sadly, many facets of Christianity have settled into a subculture mentality. Still other facets of the church have been co-opted by ideological factions, like the conservatives and the progressives and, worse, the Republicans and the Democrats.

As a result of the displacement experienced by Christians over the past fifty-plus years, Christians have pandered to and sought political power, intellectual respectability, cultural acceptance, and social affirmation—all the things Jesus couldn't care less about. As a result, the church no longer shows any semblance of serving as the host of the country. We are now the guest. The conservative impulse is to take back the country by imposing our ancient values onto the culture. The progressive impulse is to accommodate the culture, adopting the values of the spirit of the age into the church.

I recognize I am generalizing and perhaps greatly oversimplifying things in my analysis here. I am trying to make sense of my observations and much of our experience. The question Christians must grapple with in twenty-first-century America (or in any other country) is this: How might we become profoundly hospitable guests in this country? Said another way: How might we join the church Jesus is building and become again a chosen people, a royal priesthood, a holy nation, and God's special possession that we might declare the praises of him who called us out of darkness and into his marvelous light?

Here's the good news. It turns out the gospel anticipates and works best through a humble servant guest on the margins than through a show-running host in the middle. The strategy of trying to conform the culture to biblical values (meddling) without winning them to Jesus will never work. It will only generate increasing resentment and toxic culture wars in Jesus' name. The strategy of trying to accommodate the culture by changing the values of the faith (false teaching) will never work. It will only amplify human pain and brokenness in Jesus' name.

So what will work? First, loving broken people (who have no idea they are even broken) so extravagantly that they will wonder if we are affirming their lifestyle—which they would expect us to reject. The conservatives will hate us for this. Second, living in such uncompromising holiness and supernatural righteousness that it inspires awe and hunger for God. The progressives will hate us for this. And these scenarios will simultaneously create astounding power and withering persecution—honor from God and hatred from the world. This is the stuff of legend—the love of Jesus through the life of his church. The same one who said, "I will build my church," also said, "You will be my witnesses."

The Prayer

Jesus, you are the Messiah, the Son of the living God. You are the Creator Host of all creation, and yet you came to us in disguise as a humble guest. This is astonishing. You came to your own, and your own did not receive you. Your love was unreasonable and your holiness unattainable. And yet you call us to belong to you in such a fashion that you become your very self for others in and through us. Holy Spirit, fill us with the holiness of love and the love of holiness. Praying in Jesus' name. Amen.

The Questions

What do you make of this notion of Christians and the church serving as humble servant guests in their particular national context rather than trying to be the "host" with the most?

Week 7:
Discussion Questions

Hearing the Text: 1 Peter 4:7–16

The end of all things is near. Therefore be alert and of sober mind so that you may pray. Above all, love each other deeply, because love covers over a multitude of sins. Offer hospitality to one another without grumbling. Each of you should use whatever gift you have received to serve others, as faithful stewards of God's grace in its various forms. If anyone speaks, they should do so as one who speaks the very words of God. If anyone serves, they should do so with the strength God provides, so that in all things God may be praised through Jesus Christ. To him be the glory and the power for ever and ever. Amen.

Dear friends, do not be surprised at the fiery ordeal that has come on you to test you, as though something strange were happening to you. But rejoice inasmuch as you participate in the sufferings of Christ, so that you may be overjoyed when his glory is revealed. If you are insulted because of the name of Christ, you are blessed, for the Spirit of glory and of God rests on you. If you suffer, it should not be as a murderer or thief or any other kind of criminal, or even as a meddler. However, if you suffer as a Christian, do not be ashamed, but praise God that you bear that name.

Responding to the Text

- What did you hear?
- What did you see?
- What did you otherwise sense from the Lord?

Sharing Insights and Implications for Discipleship

Drawing from the Scripture text and daily readings, what did you find challenging, encouraging, provocative, comforting, invasive, inspiring, corrective, affirming, guiding, or warning?

Shaping Intentions for Prayer

Write your discipleship intention for the week ahead.

8
WEEK

---

1 Peter 4:17–5:14

---

1 Peter 4:17–19

50

Let Judgment Begin with Me

> For it is time for judgment to begin with God's household; and if it begins with us, what will the outcome be for those who do not obey the gospel of God? And,
> "If it is hard for the righteous to be saved,
> what will become of the ungodly and the sinner?"
> So then, those who suffer according to God's will should commit themselves to their faithful Creator and continue to do good.

══ Consider This ══

There is something deeply embedded in human nature that resists the whole concept of judgment. Actually, we are pretty fine with it as long as it's directed at someone else—like the ungodly and the sinner (or the conservatives or the progressives). In the minds and hearts of most people, including every one of us, the only thing worse than someone calling us out for being wrong (i.e., judgment) is admitting and owning that we are wrong.

> For it is time for judgment to begin with God's household.

Most of us will gladly say amen to Peter's word today, because we interpret it to mean "Let judgment begin with our opponents in God's household"—the ones we disagree with. We say yes to getting sin out of the camp. Whether we will admit it or not, most of us (even me) believe judgment is a phenomenon reserved for "the other," or at least someone other than me—until we read Peter's next words:

> . . . and if it begins with us . . .

"Us" is not "them." "Us" is "we," and "we" is you and me. And as far as I'm concerned, "we" must begin with "me." Here's the point: I must let judgment begin not with someone else but with me.

Remember, Peter heard this from Jesus in a live audience and probably a hundred other times in private:

> "Why do you look at the speck of sawdust in your brother's eye and pay no attention to the plank in your own eye? How can you say to your brother, 'Let me take the speck out of your eye,' when all the time there is a plank in your own eye? You hypocrite, first take the plank out of your own eye, and then you will see clearly to remove the speck from your brother's eye." (Matthew 7:3–5)

Translation: Let judgment begin with me.

Let's be clear though. Judgment is not self-condemnation. It is not self-shaming. It is humble honesty before God leading to the realignment of one's whole life according to the truth. This is why a life anchored in the Word of God and animated by the Spirit of God is utterly essential.

> Search me, God, and know my heart;
> > test me and know my anxious thoughts.
> See if there is any offensive way in me,
> > and lead me in the way everlasting. (Psalm 139:23–24)

═══ The Prayer ═══

Jesus, you are the Messiah, the Son of the living God. You are the Judge and the judgment. In fact, you have taken the judgment on yourself. You who knew no sin became sin for us, so that we might become the righteousness of God. Holy Spirit, would you search me and know my heart? Would you test me and know my anxious thoughts? See if there is any offensive way in me, and lead me in the way everlasting. All of this—that I may become the holy love of God. Praying in Jesus' name. Amen.

═══ The Questions ═══

Are you ready to let judgment begin with you? If so, how? If not, why not?

51

1 Peter 5:1–5

I Would Like to Welcome Me to the Elder Class

> *To the elders among you, I appeal as a fellow elder and a witness of Christ's sufferings who also will share in the glory to be revealed: Be shepherds of God's flock that is under your care, watching over them—not because you must, but because you are willing, as God wants you to be; not pursuing dishonest gain, but eager to serve; not lording it over those entrusted to you, but being examples to the flock. And when the Chief Shepherd appears, you will receive the crown of glory that will never fade away.*
>
> *In the same way, you who are younger, submit yourselves to your elders.*

═══ Consider This ═══

To the elders among you . . .

Much has been made over the centuries of the biblical meaning of the term *elder* and how the church should interpret it. It mostly comes down to the leadership structure of the community and the designation of a particular role or position within the community. Some churches designate their elders as their ordained leaders. Others make the elders into a type of board of governance and leadership. Whatever the case, Peter is clearly referencing some kind of leadership structure in the community, noting an official kind of entrustment of a group of people into the care of another person.

I would like to address the issue of elders with a less specific ecclesial application and a broader conceptual understanding. Interestingly, and ironically, in all the wrangling over who can be an elder and who cannot, one of the most obvious and important features of the term may have been left behind. Elder actually does mean elder. It means older. Peter, who identifies himself as a "fellow elder," is probably around sixty at the time of this letter. I recently turned fifty-five. I received a few birthday wishes, but no induction into elderhood. So today, I am officially welcoming myself into the elder class.

In celebration of my entry into elderhood, I am addressing any and every fifty-five-year-old or older person in the body of Christ. Some of you are wondering where I got the number. I just decided it—maybe with a little help from the AARP. So here's to you, members of the elder class of saints in the church Jesus is building—men and women. I address you, like Peter, as "fellow elders." I recognize I am a mere freshman member of our class of elders.

To all of us, I say it is time for us to stop lamenting the present state of affairs and step fully into the calling Jesus has for us. The calling is not to take ownership, but rather to humbly claim responsibility. There is a role and responsibility only we can and must take on in this church—a role and responsibility that does not begin with our local church. This is not primarily about getting more involved; it's about becoming more consecrated. It begins with Jesus himself. He is our first and highest calling. This is about offering as a gift the rest of our earthly lives to Jesus Messiah and the church he is building.

Local churches are very confused about old people. They think we want to fold bulletins, go on museum tours, and attend seminars on aging at the church—oh, and I almost forgot, write checks! And it's time to stop grouping us into triaged ghettos of the progressively aging. The world trends toward gathering and grouping people according to their inabilities, disabilities, and incapacities. Because the kingdom of heaven is ontologically distinct from the world, the church Jesus is building must be categorically different. Wherever and everywhere you find the church Jesus is building, it will reveal a DNA of intergenerationality, manifested in a culture of spiritual parenting and grandparenting.

We must show retirement the door. Sure, you can quit your job and even move into a retirement village, but you can't retire in the church Jesus is building. He is looking to promote you—not to be a busier volunteer, but to live out of a shepherd anointing. After sixty or seventy years, you have a flock. It may not feel like a flock, but it is. You must learn to shepherd this flock with ever-increasing wisdom, love, and encouragement to wake up to the real life. And if you don't have a flock, Jesus stands ready to entrust you with one.

And as we get admitted into the senior class of the elder years, we are being called to a demonstration of 2 Corinthians 4:16: "Therefore we do not lose heart. Though outwardly we are wasting away, yet inwardly we are being renewed day by day."

Old is good. Older is even better. Jesus has not reversed aging. He did it one better. He reversed death. And because Jesus has reversed death, the entire concept of aging has undergone a constitutional change. As elders, we must accept that it is time to step into a whole new relationship with death and dying. We have the opportunity to lead the culture in what it looks like to die well—to go out not with a whimper but in a blaze of glory, leaving a legacy of life and love. In this way, our passing will become an awakening for so many of our peers who don't yet know God—not to mention our children and their children and their children.

Come on, elders of the kingdom! You may try to dismiss me as an idealistic freshman member of the elder class. Just know, I won't stop. I'm coming for you! And let me say a word to the younger generations. Reject the false choice that in order for you to lead, the older generation must step aside. It is simultaneously a both/and. The church cannot be the church without all of the generations working in collaborative concert to declare the praises of him who called us out of darkness and into his marvelous light. How about we pursue relationship across generational lines, holding space for and giving place to one another?

===== The Prayer =====

Jesus, you are the Messiah, the Son of the living God. Thank you for the elders among us, the ones who go before, blazing the trail of sainthood. Lead us into a culture of deep honor and blessing, where the young revere the elders and the elders serve the young. Break us out of our silos of sameness and into the rich gift of the intergenerational kingdom of God. Holy Spirit, spark calling in the elders among us. Remind us that nothing is wasted. No time has been lost on your clock. You will accomplish your will. Bring us into it more fully. Praying in Jesus' name. Amen.

Are you an elder? Does this encourage you or not? Are you ready for a new vision? Are you a younger person now? How do you view becoming an elder? Will you prepare for it? What might pursuing a relationship of spiritual parenting look like for both the young and the elders?

52 | 1 Peter 5:5–6

Swing Thought #1: Humble Yourself

> *All of you, clothe yourselves with humility toward one another, because,*
> > *"God opposes the proud*
> > > *but shows favor to the humble."*
> > *Humble yourselves, therefore, under God's mighty hand, that he may lift you up in due time.*

=== **Consider This** ===

As Peter makes the turn toward home and closing this five-chapter epistle, he gives the church Jesus is building a few swing thoughts. The golfers in the house will immediately get the reference. For the rest, a swing thought is a single thought a golfer has in their mind as they stand over the ball and prepare to hit it. It can be something as simple as "Keep your head still," "Roll your wrists over at impact," or "Stay down on the ball."

The problem with swing thoughts is just that. You really can hold only one at a time. It's why back in another life when I played golf, I dismissed every thought from my mind save one, which I learned from my college golfing colleague John Daly—"Grip it and rip it!" (I know! Jack Nicklaus once told me never to drop names.)

Peter is going to give us three parting Holy Spirit swing thoughts:

(1) humble yourself; (2) don't be anxious; (3) resist Satan. My encouragement is to pick one based on your situation (i.e., the shot in front of you).

Let's focus on the first one today.

> All of you, clothe yourselves with humility toward one another.

What is humility, really? We know it when we see it, right? And we can spot a fake a mile away. It's why trying to be humble never works. There are two fundamental dynamics at play in all people: identity and image. Humility only comes from a secure sense of identity. A secure sense of identity comes from belonging to Jesus. When one does not have a secure sense of identity, all the energy goes into managing the image.

This is where pride comes in. Pride is the strategy to overcome an insecure internal identity by developing false security around one's external image. We see this everywhere in two basic expressions—enmeshed codependence and isolated independence. In plain speech—people-pleasing and high performance. (Okay, there is also virtue signaling, which is the insecure self on bad religion, aka Pharisaism, but we will save that for another day.)

Humility is not a behavior; it is the external manifestation of one's true internal identity. When Peter says, "Clothe yourselves with humility toward one another," he is saying, "Let your outside image reflect your true identity. Strip away the false image. Be your real self. Clothe yourself with humility. Cut the pretense." Here's how Paul says it: "Do not lie to each other, since you have taken off your old self with its practices and have put on the new self, which is being renewed in knowledge in the image of its Creator" (Colossians 3:9–10).

This is why a commitment to banding together matters so much. Most people remain stuck, captive to their insecure selves with all of their broken patterns and pathologies. I know I lived too many years stuck there. This is the core work of the second half of the gospel—the reclamation of a baptismal identity and the aim of doing discipleship in the context of real relationships.[1] Jesus sets captives free. He really

---

1. For an introduction to the idea of "the second half of the gospel," revisit page 17 and chapter 5.

does. It's why you must learn to believe the real truth about yourself, no matter how beautiful it is.

The Prayer

Jesus, you are the Messiah, the Son of the living God. You who are everything made yourself nothing. You are humility embodied. You clothed yourself with utter humility—and what a sight to behold! Holy Spirit, give us vision and insight into Jesus and into ourselves. We confess our insecurity in the deep places. Heal us and set us free to be who you made us to be—image bearers of you. These are the paths of true righteousness. Lead us there for your name's sake. All of this for the glory of the Father. Praying in Jesus' name. Amen.

The Questions

So are you humble? Just kidding. Are you growing in your true identity in Jesus? How so? Are you secure in deep, abiding attachment to him? How about to others?

53

1 Peter 5:7

Swing Thought #2: Displace Anxiety

> *Cast all your anxiety on him because he cares for you.*

Consider This

Today we come to swing thought number two of three. I'm not sure what to call it. I want to say, "Don't be anxious," but we all know the harder we try not to be anxious, the more anxious we often become. If it were that simple, none of us would be anxious. Anxiety is complex.

Let's talk about what the Bible means when it says "anxiety" in this instance. The word is transliterated *merimna*, and it sounds like it's spelled. It carries a meaning of dividing and fracturing a person's being into parts. Anxiety, in a very literal sense, pulls us apart. It disintegrates our very sense of self by attacking our core sense of security.

So how do we deal with anxiety?

> Cast all your anxiety on him because he cares for you.

Is it as simple as telling God what we are anxious about? It sounds good, but all too often when we are anxious, we tend to worry our prayers rather than casting our anxiety on God. Anxiety must actually be *displaced* within us. The little word *because* tells us how this displacement works. It brings us to the four most important words in today's text:

> He cares for you.

Did you hear that?
He cares for you.
I want to turn this in a very personal direction now. Repeat after me:
He cares for me.
Again.
He cares for me.
Again.
He cares for me.
Again.
He cares for me.
Okay, this is a declaration of faith. Let's take it a step further and make it an act of prayer. Repeat after me, to God:
Father, you care for me.
Again.
Jesus, you care for me.
Again.
Holy Spirit, you care for me.
The more I abide with his care-filled presence within me, the more I find his peace and security solidifying within me. Instead of worry and anxious thoughts pulling me apart at the seams, I find myself being brought together at the core of my being. This is not hard, but it does

require work. It is the work of *abiding*. It is not just believing the concept; it is entering into the truth.

Before we go, let's be clear about something important. There is garden-variety anxiety, which is what Peter seems to refer to in this text. And then there is anxiety as a serious (and sometimes severe) mental health condition. We all struggle with anxiety in the general sense. Increasingly, many people, especially the young, are suffering with anxiety at the level of an infirmity or affliction and even to the point of mental illness.

While the remedy prescribed above is apt for all anxiety, for those suffering in this more profound way, it is imperative to seek out the help of others. Anxiety is not a sin. Do not allow its presence in your life to isolate you. Reach out. Because God cares for you, there is all manner of help—even cure.

The Prayer

Jesus, you are the Messiah, the Son of the living God. You taught us not to worry or be anxious. You pointed us to the birds and the flowers and lifted our eyes to the one who cares for us—our Abba Father. Holy Spirit, we hear these things, and we kind of believe them. We need you to interpret them and even infuse them into our inmost being. Father, you care for me. Jesus, you care for me. Holy Spirit, you care for me. Praying in Jesus' name. Amen.

The Questions

What is your history and present experience with anxiety? Are you grasping this revelation of the way God works by displacement—in this instance with peace displacing anxiety? It keeps showing up. It flips the script, doesn't it?

54

1 Peter 5:8–9
Swing Thought #3: Stand Firm

> Be alert and of sober mind. Your enemy the devil prowls around like a
> roaring lion looking for someone to devour. Resist him, standing firm
> in the faith, because you know that the family of believers throughout
> the world is undergoing the same kind of sufferings.

══ Consider This ══

God's people all over the world are going through trials and sufferings
all the time. Some of it is direct evil and demonic persecution delivered
through human agency. Some of it is a kind of spiritual warfare coming
from demonic attack, often exploiting the vulnerabilities common to
us all, like human brokenness, generational sin, relational dysfunction,
infirmity, and affliction. Much of it comes through the demonic strategy of pride (image management) born of insecure attachments at the
core of our being and manifesting itself through all manner of anxiety
arising from a worldview anchored in scarcity and existential fear. (This
is why we drink, smoke, overeat, hoard resources, and otherwise stay
professionally distracted.) But I digress.

Each one of us is dealing with something right now, or we are trying
to help someone else who is dealing with something—or both. Peter's
coaching here is nothing less than prescient "for the facing of this hour,"
as the hymnwriter writes.[2] As I began working through 1 Peter 5:5–9,
I thought Peter was giving us a few different closing swing thoughts. I
am now convinced the Holy Spirit is revealing to us how faith works.

Here's what I'm getting at: as we draw into our core being and welcome Jesus to form, transform, and nourish our true identity (humility),
he fills us with his Spirit, who displaces anxiety with deep attachment
becoming security—and from this place of deep security we learn to
stand firm in "the faith," resist evil (via the world, the flesh, and the
devil), and move in the world through the otherworldly power of love.

Jesus is building his church, which is a veritable seedbed of this
kind of life formation. This doesn't really happen in isolation, but rather
in banded fellowship. Persons don't become a people through buying

---

2. Harry Emerson Fosdick, "God of Grace and God of Glory" (1930). Public domain.

more books and learning more information and trying harder to be a better version of their old selves. We become a people by sharing deeply in one another's lives, learning to love one another and be loved by one another into our true selves and our real lives.

This is the chosen people, the royal priesthood, the holy nation, and God's special possession. Indeed, this church Jesus is building is God's special possession in all the world, for this is how God saves the world.

Did you catch the power phrase in today's text?

> Resist him, standing firm in the faith.

We don't resist evil by trying harder to resist evil. Resisting evil has a way of making evil more of a reference point. What we most need is a new point of reference, a new center of gravity if you will. That's what repentance actually is—a shifting of the center of gravity. We resist the unholy trinity of evil—the world, the flesh, and the devil—by standing firm in the faith. When our undivided focus is on "the faith," we find evil losing its grip on us. We are, as they would say in the old days, "seized by the power of a great affection."

Notice something else. The text does not say to stand firm in *our* faith; it says to stand firm in *the* faith. Our faith can rise and fall like the tides; *the* faith never fails or fades. We want to learn to stand firm in *the* faith, as Scripture says, "that was once for all entrusted to God's holy people" (Jude 3). Because *our* faith can wax and wane and be subject to the vicissitudes and vexations of our circumstances, we must regularly and relentlessly rehearse *the* faith. This is precisely why the Holy Spirit has gifted the church Jesus is building with the great creeds. They are the crystallized confessions of *the* faith.

How about we rehearse "the faith" now by proclaiming together the ancient declaration we know as the Apostles' Creed.

> I believe in God the Father Almighty,
> maker of heaven and earth;
> and in Jesus Christ, his only Son, our Lord:

who was conceived by the Holy Spirit,
born of the Virgin Mary,
suffered under Pontius Pilate,
was crucified, dead, and buried;
he descended into hell.
The third day he rose again from the dead;
he ascended into heaven,
and sits at the right hand of God the Father
Almighty;
from there he shall come to judge the living and
the dead.
I believe in the Holy Spirit,
the holy catholic Church,
the communion of saints,
the forgiveness of sins,
the resurrection of the body,
and the life everlasting. Amen.

The Prayer

Jesus, you are the Messiah, the Son of the living God. Today we want to stand still and behold the deliverance of our God. As you were lifted up on the cross, you delivered us from sin, death, and darkness. Indeed, you parted the sea so we could walk through it, drowning our fears in your perfect love. Holy Spirit, bring us into the inside of this redemption today like never before. We don't want a better version of our old life; we want the new creation life in fullness. Praying in Jesus' name. Amen.

The Questions

How is the trial or suffering you are presently enduring shaping your faith, drawing you into core attachment to Jesus, displacing anxiety, and strengthening the perseverance of love in you? Are you seeing the difference between *our* faith and *the* faith?

55 | 1 Peter 5:10–14

The Great Prison Break

> And the God of all grace, who called you to his eternal glory in Christ, after you have suffered a little while, will himself restore you and make you strong, firm and steadfast. To him be the power for ever and ever. Amen.
>
> With the help of Silas, whom I regard as a faithful brother, I have written to you briefly, encouraging you and testifying that this is the true grace of God. Stand fast in it.
>
> She who is in Babylon, chosen together with you, sends you her greetings, and so does my son Mark. Greet one another with a kiss of love.
>
> Peace to all of you who are in Christ.

=== **Consider This** ===

I wonder if Peter was thinking about the time he was in prison as he closed out his letter to the scattered exiles whom he called the chosen people, the royal priesthood, the holy nation, and God's special possession. I wonder if he was remembering the night he sat bound between two soldiers in a dank prison cell guarded by multiple sentries. It was the eve of his trial before Herod and a certain execution. His best friend James had already met the executioner's sword. Hear the story from Luke's pen:

> So Peter was kept in prison, but the church was earnestly praying to God for him.
>
> The night before Herod was to bring him to trial, Peter was sleeping between two soldiers, bound with two chains, and sentries stood guard at the entrance. Suddenly an angel of the Lord appeared and a light shone in the cell. He struck Peter on the side and woke him up. "Quick, get up!" he said, and the chains fell off Peter's wrists. (Acts 12:5–7)

If you have a few more minutes today and want to be astonished, read the rest of Acts 12. Within the week, not only had Peter not been executed, but also Herod had been struck dead by God. And for good measure, you might take a look at Acts 16:16–40 and the story of Silas, Peter's friend, and his miraculous bail from jail.

It is easy to read these stories from the far side of redemption, from the promise side of the promised land. We have to put ourselves in their shoes (or stocks, as was the case at the time)—on the uncertain side of trial and under the threat of tragedy. Many reading today sit in these same sorts of prison cells. Though the circumstances vary, the chains all hold the same. Maybe it is the trial of the untimely loss of a loved one. Perhaps it is the crushing death of a marriage and the ruins of what was once a happy family. It could be the curse of cancer or some other sickness that will not relent. For some, it seems like a slow-motion train wreck, spanning years and even a decade or more—one unforeseen disaster after another—and all of it unfolding while they have done their dead-level best to stand firm in the faith and obey Jesus every step of the way. They are somewhere between resignation and more resolve, and they know neither will help.

Peter knows we need a better prescription. In his final words he scratches out a sketch of hope. Yes, Peter knew of what he spoke when he closed his letter with this word of hope. I invite you to take courage in it:

> And the God of all grace, who called you to his eternal glory in Christ, after you have suffered a little while, will himself restore you and make you strong, firm and steadfast. To him be the power for ever and ever. Amen.

It all points us to Jesus, the Lord of the church he is building, who lay in that dank prison cell of a borrowed tomb, bound in graveclothes, his body still shackled in the curse he had just crushed—as he preached the gospel to the dead who were bound in the prison of hell. And all of this as the angels warmed up for the ultimate Hallelujah Chorus: "Where, O death, is your victory? Where, O death, is your sting?" (1 Corinthians 15:55).

All of this calls to mind the fourth stanza of the great anthem of awakening "And Can It Be," penned by the poet laureate of the Great Awakening himself, Charles Wesley:

> Long my imprisoned spirit lay
> Fast bound in sin and nature's night;
> Thine eye diffused a quick'ning ray,
> I woke, the dungeon flamed with light;
> My chains fell off, my heart was free;
> I rose, went forth, and followed Thee.[3]

Sing it if you know it.

The Prayer

Jesus, you are the Messiah, the Son of the living God. Thank you for Peter, the impetuous disciple, the unlikely apostle, the first and greatest pope of the church you are building. We celebrate him today in the communion of saints, that great cloud of witnesses cheering us on. Thank you for Peter's suffering and his cross and his martyr's blood that still cries out. Thank you for your suffering, your cross, your grave, your resurrection, your ascension, your reign, and your impending return. Holy Spirit, interpret these verities and these mysteries to our deepest selves. You have our confession. You have our very lives. Build your church. Father, it will be an honor to suffer for you. Praying in Jesus' name. Amen.

The Questions

So what are the takeaways from Peter's letter? What do you remember from the journey? What has shifted in your soul?

---

3. Charles Wesley, "And Can It Be That I Should Gain" (1738). Public domain.

Week 8:
Discussion Questions

Hearing the Text: 1 Peter 4:17–5:14

For it is time for judgment to begin with God's household; and if it begins with us, what will the outcome be for those who do not obey the gospel of God? And,

> *"If it is hard for the righteous to be saved,*
> *what will become of the ungodly and the sinner?"*

So then, those who suffer according to God's will should commit themselves to their faithful Creator and continue to do good.

To the elders among you, I appeal as a fellow elder and a witness of Christ's sufferings who also will share in the glory to be revealed: Be shepherds of God's flock that is under your care, watching over them—not because you must, but because you are willing, as God wants you to be; not pursuing dishonest gain, but eager to serve; not lording it over those entrusted to you, but being examples to the flock. And when the Chief Shepherd appears, you will receive the crown of glory that will never fade away.

In the same way, you who are younger, submit yourselves to your elders. All of you, clothe yourselves with humility toward one another, because,

> *"God opposes the proud*
> *but shows favor to the humble."*

Humble yourselves, therefore, under God's mighty hand, that he may lift you up in due time. Cast all your anxiety on him because he cares for you.

Be alert and of sober mind. Your enemy the devil prowls around like a roaring lion looking for someone to devour. Resist him, standing firm in the faith, because you know that the family of believers throughout the world is undergoing the same kind of sufferings.

And the God of all grace, who called you to his eternal glory in Christ, after you have suffered a little while, will himself restore you and make you strong, firm and steadfast. To him be the power for ever and ever. Amen.

With the help of Silas, whom I regard as a faithful brother, I have written to you briefly, encouraging you and testifying that this is the true grace of God. Stand fast in it.

She who is in Babylon, chosen together with you, sends you her greetings, and so does my son Mark. Greet one another with a kiss of love.

Peace to all of you who are in Christ.

Responding to the Text

- What did you hear?
- What did you see?
- What did you otherwise sense from the Lord?

Sharing Insights and Implications for Discipleship

Drawing from the Scripture text and daily readings, what did you find challenging, encouraging, provocative, comforting, invasive, inspiring, corrective, affirming, guiding, or warning?

Shaping Intentions for Prayer

Write your discipleship intention for the week ahead.

Conclusion

As we bid farewell to the apostle Peter and thank him for the gift of his letter, I am reminded of another witness who stood in the line of Peter only a hundred years later. As Peter undoubtedly preached the greatest sermon of the first century and perhaps of all time, this witness preached what is perhaps the greatest sermon of the second century. It turns out to be the first sermon (outside of Scripture) we have on record. It is known to history as *On Pascha* and was preached by Melito, bishop of Sardis, who was one of the prominent figures of second-century Christianity.

The excerpt below was written in the year of our Lord 167. It carries a creedal essence. It is a declaration of "*the* faith," the gospel from which "our faith" flourishes. We live in a day when we need something beyond popular preachers and their ephemeral podcasts. We need durable hope from ancient proclaimers. We need the words that stirred the martyrs and consoled their mothers. If we would step out of the shallows of our time, we must have the deep-end faith of the saints to stir us. I am delighted to leave you with this profoundly stirring sermon, the likes of which most of us have never heard, much less fathomed. Read it aloud that it might have the possibility of entering not just through your brain but through your skin and into your very bones.

I give you *On Pascha* from Melito of Sardis, who gives us Jesus:

> This is the one who comes from heaven onto the
>   earth for the suffering one,
> and wraps himself in the suffering one through a
>   virgin womb
> and comes as a man.
> He accepted the suffering of the suffering one,
> through suffering in a body which could suffer,

and set free the flesh from suffering.
Through the spirit which cannot die
he slew the manslayer death.
He is the one led like a lamb
and slaughtered like a sheep;
he ransomed us from the worship of the world
as from the land of Egypt,
and he set us free from the slavery of the devil
as from the hand of Pharaoh,
and sealed our souls with his own spirit,
and the members of our body with his blood.
This is the one who clad death in shame
and, as Moses did to Pharaoh,
made the devil grieve.
This is the one who struck down lawlessness
and made injustice childless,
as Moses did to Egypt.
This is the one who delivered us from slavery to
      freedom,
from darkness into light,
from death into life,
from tyranny into an eternal Kingdom,
and made us a new priesthood,
and a people everlasting for himself.
This is the Pascha of our salvation:
this is the one who in many people endured many
      things.
This is the one who was murdered in Abel,
tied up in Isaac,
exiled in Jacob,
sold in Joseph,
exposed in Moses,
slaughtered in the lamb,
hunted down in David,
dishonored in the prophets.
This is the one made flesh in a virgin

who was hanged on a tree,
who was buried in the earth,
who was raised from the dead,
who was exalted to the heights of heaven.
This is the lamb slain,
this is the speechless lamb,
this is the one born of Mary the fair ewe,
this is the one taken from the flock,
and led to slaughter.
Who was sacrificed in the evening,
and buried at night;
who was not broken on the tree,
who was not undone in the earth,
who rose from the dead and resurrected
       humankind from the grave below. . . .
O mystifying murder! O mystifying injustice!
The master is obscured by his body exposed,
and is not held worthy of a veil to shield him
       from view.
For this reason the great lights turned away,
and the day was turned to darkness;
to hide the one denuded on the tree,
obscuring not the body of the Lord but human eyes.
For when the people did not tremble, the earth
       shook.
When the people did not fear, the heavens were
       afraid.
When the people did not rend their garments, the
       angel rent his own.
When the people did not lament, the Lord
       thundered from heaven,
and the most high gave voice. . . .
"Who takes issue with me? Let him stand
       before me.
I set free the condemned.
I gave life to the dead.

I raise up the entombed.
Who will contradict me?"
"It is I," says the Christ,
"I am he who destroys death
and triumphs over the enemy,
and crushes Hades,
and binds the strong man,
and bears humanity off to the heavenly heights."
"It is I," says the Christ.
"So come all families of people,
adulterated with sin,
and receive forgiveness of sins.
For I am your freedom.
I am the Passover of salvation,
I am the lamb slaughtered for you,
I am your ransom,
I am your life,
I am your light,
I am your salvation,
I am your resurrection,
I am your King.
I shall raise you up by my right hand,
I will lead you to the heights of heaven,
there shall I show you the everlasting father."
He it is who made the heaven and the earth,
and formed humanity in the beginning,
who was proclaimed through the law and the
        prophets,
who took flesh from a virgin,
who was hung on a tree,
who was buried in earth,
who was raised from the dead,
and ascended to the heights of heaven,
who sits at the right hand of the father,
who has the power to save all things,

through whom the father acted from the beginning
and forever.
This is the alpha and omega,
this is the beginning and the end.
the ineffable beginning and the
incomprehensible end.
This is the Christ,
this is the King,
this is Jesus,
this is the commander,
this is the Lord,
this is he who rose from the dead,
this is he who sits at the right hand of the father,
he bears the father and is borne by him.
To him be the glory and the might forever.
Amen.[1]

Wake up, sleeper, rise from the dead,
and Christ will shine on you.

---

1. Melito of Sardis, *On Pascha* (ca. AD 167; repr., Crestwood, NY: St. Vladimir's Seminary Press, 2001), 54–67.